QUIT GETTING SCREWED

QUT

GETTING

SCREWED

Understanding and Negotiating the Subcontract

KARALYNN CROMEENS

LIONCREST
PUBLISHING

QUIT GETTING SCREWED
Understanding and Negotiating the Subcontract

ISBN 978-1-5445-1774-2 *Hardcover*
      978-1-5445-1773-5 *Paperback*
      978-1-5445-1772-8 *Ebook*

For Brad, my best friend and partner forever.

CONTENTS

INTRODUCTION 11

1. THE BID 17
   *Your bid is a detailed explanation of the work you agreed to
   provide, but it does not become part of your subcontract.*

2. SUBCONTRACT DOCUMENTS 25
   *The subcontract is not the only document that describes
   what your obligations to the general contractor are.*

3. SUBCONTRACTOR BONDS 35
   Danger! Danger! Danger!

4. SCOPE OF WORK 47
   *The scope of work described in the subcontract is not the same as
   what was in your bid; review the scope documents in the proposed
   subcontract as if you were reviewing a new project to bid.*

5. DO NOT SIGN A PERSONAL GUARANTEE 55
   *The importance of being incorporated and
   not signing the personal guarantee.*

6. PRIOR WORK AND FIELD CONDITIONS 65
    These sneaky provisions need to be considered and negotiated
    before you sign the subcontract or you will be responsible
    for the work of the subcontractor before you, and you must
    visit the project site before you sign the subcontract.

7. SUBMITTALS AND AS BUILTS 73
    These are helpful tools that are required by most
    subcontracts, and they can actually help limit
    your liability should something go wrong.

8. DAILY REPORTS 83
    These are great tools to tell your side of the story
    as it happens if there are any issues.

9. PAY WHEN PAID CLAUSES 89
    Understand what a pay when paid clause is and how to defeat them.

10. RETAINAGE 97
    What retainage is and why it matters.

11. WHEN CAN I FILE A LIEN? 103
    No matter what the subcontract says, you always have the
    right to file a lien, but you must follow the proper procedure.

12. LIEN WAIVERS 107
    There is a state form and process for lien waivers. Never
    sign an unconditional waiver if you have not been paid.

13. TRUST FUNDS.. 121
    Trust funds are the payments on construction projects and must
    be paid to the people who supply labor and material to the project.

14. CHANGE ORDERS 127
    Don't work for free; make sure you have a signed
    change order before you do any extra work.

15. ASSIGNMENTS 137
*There are two different types of assignments; understand
what they are and why they matter to you.*

16. DELAY DAMAGES 145
*The schedule you provide will be used against you; understand
how dangerous being behind schedule really is.*

17. WARRANTIES 153
*Know where to find all of the terms of the warranty you
are agreeing to and how to negotiate these terms.*

18. DEFAULT AND TERMINATION 159
*What is considered a default, how it can be cured, and who has
the right to terminate the contract and for what grounds?*

19. ATTORNEY FEES AND COSTS 167
*Love us or hate us, you need to make sure this is
properly addressed in your subcontract.*

20. DISPUTE RESOLUTION 173
*Understand the difference between mediation, arbitration,
and litigation. Evaluate the pros and cons for each*

CONCLUSION 183

ACKNOWLEDGMENTS 189

ABOUT THE AUTHOR 191

INTRODUCTION

Are you tired of being a general contractor's bitch?

I hate to break it to you, but that is what you become every time you sign a subcontract you have not read or do not understand. I know, I know. Subcontracts are dense and hard to understand, and you need the job, so without reading the thing, you excitedly sign so you can get that paycheck.

Unfortunately, it doesn't always work out that way. In fact, depending on what's in the contract, you could be agreeing to cover ridiculous expenses completely outside of your skillset or services.

I've seen this happen on too many occasions to count. In the sixteen years I've practiced construction, real estate, and business law, I have reviewed and explained thousands of subcontracts. I have tried to save companies that have signed problematic subcontracts, but by the time they came to me, it was too late. There was nothing I could do to help. As hard as I fought, I could not get them out of the poisonous, one-sided subcontract they had signed.

I hated feeling helpless for these hardworking individuals. I hated seeing my clients in legal disputes over the smallest of details. I hated seeing my clients lose money—sometimes their entire business—over language they did not understand.

Most of all, I hated seeing my clients become some general contractor's bitch.

I thus realized the best way I could help was to educate subcontractors *before* they signed a subcontract—to give them the necessary tools to understand and negotiate a fair subcontract. That's why I wrote this book.

My aim with this book is to give you confidence in signing subcontracts so that you can mitigate the risks and protect your company. I wrote this book because I want you to quit getting screwed.

WHAT YOU'LL LEARN

In the pages that follow, I will share some horrifying, true stories and how you can avoid finding yourself in similar situations. I will show examples of tricky language commonly found in subcontracts, as well as what you should replace them with. I will also share some best practices that will help you if you do ever find yourself in a court of law. This book is written from the perspective of Texas law. Everything in this book is good general information, but my experience with the law is only in the state of Texas.

I dedicated a chapter to each of the following parts of a subcontract, explaining what each means, why they're important, and what you should do to protect yourself before signing any piece of paper:

- The Bid
- Subcontract Documents
- Subcontractor Bonds
- Scope of Work
- Personal Guarantees (and why you should *never* sign one)
- Prior Work and Field Conditions
- Submittals and As Builts
- Daily Reports
- Pay When Paid
- Retainage

- When You Can File a Lien
- Lien Waivers
- Trust Funds
- Change Orders
- Assignments
- Delay Damages
- Warranties
- Default and Termination
- Attorney Fees and Costs
- Dispute Resolution

By the end of the book, you will be equipped with the ability to properly evaluate your risks and negotiate your next subcontract with greater confidence and ease.

MY BACKGROUND

I come from a blue-collar background—or what I like to call the "get shit done" tribe. In this tribe, we worked with our hands, and we used our physical abilities to create and produce things. My father and my grandparents on his side were midwestern farmers, and let me just say, you do not know a hard day's work until you have worked a day on a farm. My mom was a florist, a waitress, and whatever else it took to keep her three kids fed. My mom's side of the family was (and still is) full of subcontractors. My grandfather moved dirt and built golf courses, one of my uncles and my brother own irrigation companies, and another uncle is an electrical subcontractor. Our families have relied on what we produced for survival.

While I was in law school, my husband and I started a material supply company that sold mostly to subcontractors. In the beginning, it was just the two of us running the company. He made the deliveries and I ran the warehouse. I had never worked so hard in my life. We worked endless sixty-hour weeks, always hustling to get the next sale. Despite its various challenges, however, I would not change it for the world. It taught me how excruciatingly difficult and stressful it is to start your own company. For example, it taught me how—despite putting in our time, energy, and effort to complete a job—if the check for that project did not come when it was supposed to, we were not going to make payroll for our people, let alone ourselves. We made a lot of sacrifices to build the company during this time.

As subcontractors, I know you make sacrifices too.

My experience also made me realize that when issues arise or you have legal questions regarding your company, you need action and answers immediately—you cannot wait. This inspired me to create a law firm that subcontractors and material suppliers can count on every time they call. So I did. I have taken all of my experiences and built the law firm I would want as a material supplier and subcontractor. I'm proud to say we will always answer your call and never make you wait three or four days for a response.

The Cromeens Law Firm, PLLC, has helped thousands of subcontractors understand subcontracts and strengthen their business as a whole.

I wrote this book to help subcontractors protect the sacrifices they have made by starting and growing their own companies. These sacrifices, including the thousands of hours away from their families, deserve to be protected. You should not have to risk everything just to be able to make a living.

With the knowledge and insight you'll gain through the chapters that follow, I hope your hands will no longer get sweaty with nervousness when negotiating your next job. I hope your heart no longer races as you look over the sometimes-confusing language found in subcontracts.

Most importantly, I hope you never sign a subcontract that puts you out of business.

We'll start where all subcontractors start when looking for work: the bid.

CHAPTER 1

THE BID

"I did not agree to do the electrical work. I never agree to do the electrical work."

That's what Josh from Super Door Subcontractor told me after the general contractor on his community college project had sent him a notice of default letter. The letter demanded that he return to the project site and install the electrical components for the glass doors he had just finished installing. The letter further stated that if the requested work was not completed in the next forty-eight hours, Josh's subcontract would be terminated.

"I'm a door contractor, not an electrical contractor. I didn't agree to do the electrical components," Josh said.

"Have you looked at the scope that was referenced in the subcontract you signed?" I asked.

"No, but I didn't put the electrical components as part of my bid. If I have to install the electrical components, I will lose my ass. I didn't budget for that," Josh explained.

Sure enough, after we reviewed the paperwork, Josh's bid did not include the electrical components, but the scope of work Josh agreed to when he signed the subcontract did.

The best advice I could give Josh was to hire someone to install the electrical components. If he did not, the general contractor would terminate Josh's contract. Once the subcontract was terminated, the general contractor had no obligation to pay Josh for the work he had already done. As unfair as that sounds, that's what Josh signed up for: he wouldn't get a dime until *all* the work in his scope was completed.

If Josh didn't complete his scope of work, the general contractor would hire someone to install the electrical components and back charge Josh for that expense. More often than not, the replacement subcontractor is never as reasonable as what you could find. And if that wasn't bad enough, if the general contractor had to finish Josh's scope, there would be an additional 15% added to the actual cost of the electrical components to cover the general contractor's administrative fee.

Josh ended up taking my advice and hired someone to

install the electrical components, costing him $3,000. Although Josh did not make money on that project, the cost could have been exponential if he had not finished.

WHAT IS A BID?

A bid is an offer you send to the general contractor saying that you will do the work described for a certain price. A scope is what is attached to the subcontract and describes the work you are hired to do. (We'll dive deeper into a scope in chapter 4.) Your bid and the scope attached to the subcontract are rarely the same. More importantly, your bid will not become part of the subcontract. Every time you receive a subcontract to sign, you need to review the scope as if you were reviewing a new project to bid.

When you prepare your bid, make sure you review all the documents in the bid package, including required plans and specifications. If you have questions, ask the general contractor. Then gather the information you need to get an accurate estimate of how much it will cost you to complete your scope of work. When you submit your bid, ensure that it includes an itemized list of everything you agree to work on. Include specifics, such as square footage and the grade of materials you are proposing to use. It is important to be clear what the price for your scope of work includes.

ITEMIZE YOUR BIDS

There are two main types of bid proposal methods. The first is the itemized method, which lists exactly what you agree to do for the reflected price. The second method is when you generally reference the scope of work for a stated price.

I highly recommend that you always itemize your bids.

A bid is a legal offer that can be accepted once it is provided to the general contractor. If the bid you sent is not itemized and is missing something, it could mean financial ruin. For example, let's say you are an HVAC subcontractor, and you receive a request to bid a rehab facility. You submit a bid that isn't itemized, simply stating that you will do the HVAC work on the rehab facility for $300,000. The general contractor reviews the bids for the HVAC work, and your bid stands out because it is about $100,000 lower than the other subcontractors' bids. It is clear you missed something in the bid. The general contractor immediately sends you a subcontract before you realize your mistake. You can withdraw your offer before it is accepted, but once the general contractor sends you that email stating that your offer is accepted, you cannot back out. You are now on the hook for an additional $100,000 worth of work you did not budget for. What would that do to your company?

If you had sent an itemized bid, it would have been clear

what you were agreeing to do for your $300,000 offer and that you were not offering to do the whole scope for the $300,000. Now, if the general contractor sends you an email accepting your offer, you are only on the hook to do what was in the bid—thanks to your itemized list.

What if the general contractor sends you a subcontract that includes the whole scope for your $300,000 price? If you are in the habit of reviewing the scope attached to every subcontract as if it were a new bid (which I encourage you to do!), you will catch that the scope is larger than what your bid included. If this should ever happen to you, *do not* sign the subcontract, and immediately contact the general contractor. Let them know that the extra work was not included in your bid, and if they need you to do this additional work, it will cost $100,000 more. Boom! Crisis averted.

Missing something in the scope does not only happen because you miss something when you are putting your bid together. Project requirements often change in between the time you bid the project and receive the subcontract. There could be a new version of the plans that alter the project, or an RFI (request for information) could change your scope of work.

It is thus of the utmost importance for you to always read the scope as if you were reviewing a new project to bid.

And while I'm at it, make sure your bid is professionally written, meaning there aren't any errors or typos. The bid should speak for itself; everything should be detailed and clearly explained. You are more likely to be hired if your bid is complete and easy to understand.

LEARN THESE TWO THINGS

If you learn anything from this book, learn these two things: first, make sure your bid is accurate and done in the itemized method. Your bid is a legal offer and can be accepted as is once it is sent. Second, every time you receive a subcontract for a new project, review the scope as if you are bidding a new project, and compare that price with your original bid for the project.

If the price you get for the scope attached to the subcontract is higher than your bid, find out what the difference is. Once you have found the discrepancy, send the general contractor an email that says something to the effect of: "My original bid did not include [list everything it didn't include here]. If you would like me to do [list them again], the subcontract price will need to be raised to $[enter your new dollar amount]. Please send over a revised subcontract for that amount. Thank you."

Had Josh taken the time to review the scope attached to his subcontract, he would have seen that it was different from the bid he submitted and would have saved himself some money. Do not be like Josh. Take the time to review the scope before you sign a subcontract.

You have not even signed a subcontract yet and are already facing grave danger. The real fun begins when we dive into what documents make up the subcontract, which we'll address in the next chapter.

KEY POINTS

- Your bid does not become part of the subcontract.
- Always submit an itemized bid.
- Your bid is a legal offer and can be accepted once it is provided to the general contractor, so make sure it is correct.

CHAPTER 2

———

SUBCONTRACT DOCUMENTS

The first rule about subcontracts is...*there are no rules.* Whatever you sign in a subcontract will be used against you.

"What do you mean I have to pay delay damages of $500 per day for every day the completion date is delayed? That was not in my contract," exclaimed Amy, from Super Painting Subcontractor.

"Well, it wasn't in your subcontract, but you did agree to it," I explained.

"I don't understand," sighed Amy.

"In your subcontract, it incorporates the terms of the prime contract, the contract between the owner and the general contractor. That contract has liquidated damages of $500 per day for every day the completion date is delayed. The demand letter you received from your general contractor claims that your company is responsible for the completion date being delayed by fifty days, which means you owe them $25,000."

Because the prime contract had become part of Amy's subcontract—even though she had never seen that document, let alone read it—she agreed to its stipulation of paying a $500-per-day penalty for not completing the project on time. Since it took her company fifty days after the date of completion, Amy had to pay the $25,000.

Sounds unfair, doesn't it? Unfortunately, there is no set of laws or rules in place to protect you and guarantee that the subcontract is fair. In fact, most of the subcontracts I have read are not fair, are one-sided, and do not favor the subcontractor.

The subcontract itself is not the only document that you will be held responsible for. Generally, the subcontract is made up of the following documents:

- Subcontract
- Prime contract

- Plans
- Specifications
- Project schedule

Notice what is not on the list: *your bid*. Once you sign the subcontract documents, your bid cannot be used to describe the work you were hired to do. Only the documents contained in the subcontract documents will be used.

In this chapter, we will review these documents, where the dangers are, and how to avoid them.

THE PRIME CONTRACT

The prime contract is the contract between the owner and the general contractor. In my opinion, making the prime contract part of the subcontract is BS. What job does the general contractor have if you have to be responsible for its obligations to the owner? They have none of the risk but get all of the rewards. Oh, and by the way, you will be held responsible for all of the terms of the prime contract but not receive any of the benefits, which means that you cannot sue the owner directly for breach of contract, nor can you have a constitution lien by saying that you have a direct contract with the owner.

The clause that incorporates the prime contract will normally be toward the front of the subcontract and will generally look something like this:

> *Subcontractor agrees to abide by all the "Contract Documents" Contract Documents means (i) this subcontract (ii) the Prime Contract (iii) all general, supplementary, and other conditions applicable to the project, (iv) the drawings and specifications, and (v) all standards, requirements, or conditions incorporated into the Contract Documents by reference.*

Here is another example of what it might look like:

> *To the extent of the Agreement between Owner and Contractor (Prime Agreement) applies to the Work of Subcontractor, Subcontractor assumes toward Contractor all obligations, rights, duties and redress that Contractor assumes toward Owner and others under the Prime Agreement. In the event of conflicts or inconsistencies between provisions of this Agreement and the prime Agreement, this Agreement shall govern. Prime Agreement will be made available upon Subcontractor's request.*

The best-case scenario is for this provision to be removed, but general contractors are unlikely to remove the incorporation of the prime contract. In that case, here are some ways you can better protect yourself.

1. **Request a copy of the prime contract.** How can you, in good faith, bind yourself to a document you have never seen, let alone read? Before you sign the subcontract, request a copy of the prime contract and any change orders that have been issued. Review the prime contract and change orders to make sure that you are not agreeing to something more than what you agreed to in the subcontract.

2. **Have the general contractor assign you its rights to payment for your scope of work.** The suggested language would look something like this: *"General Contractor hereby assigns its rights to payment for Subcontractor's scope of Work under the Prime Contract to Subcontractor. Subcontractor shall have the same rights to payment and remedies for nonpayment as the General Contractor has against Owner."*

The second suggestion will give you constitutional lien rights (which have more leverage than your lien rights as a subcontractor) just like the general contractor has. It will also give you the right to sue the owner directly for breach of contract. If you are going to have the same responsibilities as the general contractor, you should have the same rights as well.

Asking for the prime contract to be removed from your subcontract is not an unreasonable request. Attorneys have added the prime contract to the terms of the subcontract as a "catchall." Just in case the attorney forgot some term or obligation in the subcontract, it would be picked up by the prime contract. Asking that all of your obligations to the general contractor only be in the subcontract is not an unreasonable request.

I cannot tell you whether the general contractor will change or remove the provision making the prime contract part of the subcontract. What I can tell you is that I've had clients who have been financially harmed by the terms of the prime contract because they did not realize that they had agreed to what was found therein.

My goal is to tell you where the risks are. It is your job to decide what risk your company is willing to take.

THE PLANS AND SPECIFICATIONS

The plans and specifications, in the most basic terms, are the directions on how to build the project. Each scope of work will have a particular set of plans and specifications to follow. Make sure the same set of plans that you based your bid on are the ones attached to the subcontract. Make sure they have the same date and that you read any bulletins, addenda, or requests for information (RFI) issued since you bid the project.

PROJECT SCHEDULE

Normally, the subcontract will have the project schedule as an exhibit/attachment. Review this closely to ensure that they have given you enough time to complete your scope of work. Do not wait to look at this until after you sign the subcontract. Liquidated and/or delayed damages will be based on this schedule. Do not agree to a schedule you cannot complete. Before you sign the subcontract, have the schedule changed to a time frame you know you can complete.

FIND THE LIST

Although we went over the most common documents in a subcontract, there could be others. In order to determine what documents are part of your agreement with the general contractor, you need to read the subcontract and look for the list. It will be in there. Sometimes it has its own heading, like this:

Article 1 the Subcontract Document

The subcontract documents consist of (1) this Subcontract Agreement; (2) the Prime Contract (the contract between the owner and General Contractor); (3) the Plans and specifications dated 12-1-2019; (4) Modifications issued subsequent to the Prime Contract, whether before or after the execution of this Agreement; and (5) Modifications to the subcontract.

The statement of the subcontract documents can also be less obvious and look something like this:

The Prime Contract and the following schedules and attachments are incorporated by reference and made part of this Agreement: Schedule A Plans and specifications; Schedule B Guarantee; Schedule C Contract items; Schedule D Project schedule and Schedule F–K Subcontractor procedures.

In addition to the four documents we highlighted, the subcontract itself will state that you have read and understood the subcontract and all subcontract documents. It will further state that there are no oral agreements outside these written documents; the written documents are the whole agreement between you and the general contractor. This means that whatever someone might have *told* you will not be part of your agreement and that your only agreement is what is in writing. What someone might have *told* you does not mean anything.

Take the time to read the subcontract and all of the subcontract documents. Get a copy of the prime contract before you agree to its terms. This will take work and is not easy, but the survival of your company depends on it.

If you have questions, ask the general contractor; general contractors are impressed by informed questions. Had Amy requested a copy of the prime contract and read it, she could have negotiated her way out of the ridiculous late penalty of $500 a day and saved her company $25,000.

There is no one out there watching your back when it comes to what you agree to in your subcontract. You are the only one who can do that. In the next chapter, we'll go over how to watch your back when it comes to subcontractor bonds.

KEY POINTS

- The subcontract is not the only document you are responsible for.
- Do not just agree to the prime contract being part of your subcontract. Request a copy of the prime contract and add language to make sure you get the benefits of the prime contract, not just the responsibilities.
- Make sure the same set of plans and specifications that you based your bid on are the ones attached to the subcontract.
- Do not agree to a schedule you cannot complete.

CHAPTER 3

———

SUBCONTRACTOR BONDS

Super AC Subcontractor was awarded their biggest sub-contract ever: $3 million.

All they had to do before starting was to obtain a payment bond and a performance bond for the full amount of its subcontract. This was a requirement, so they did it. After they got the required bonds, they signed the subcontract and couldn't wait to get to work.

The project went great at first, but eventually, Super AC Subcontractor realized that it could not complete the project for the subcontract price. After Super AC Sub-contractor reviewed the scope of work agreed to in the subcontract, it turned out they were about $250,000 short in the subcontract price because they missed something in the bid. Super AC Subcontractor took a hard look at their finances and searched for ways they could use the money they had to finish the project, even though the project would be a huge loss. After a careful review of their books, Super AC Subcontractor determined that finishing the project would actually put them out of business. They couldn't finish the project without additional funds from the general contractor for their scope of work.

Super AC Subcontractor approached the general contractor, explained the issue, and begged for additional funds to finish the project. The general contractor ignored the request. At this point, it became clear to Super AC Subcontractor that the only reason they were hired was because their bid was at least $250,000 lower than the other bids the general contractor received.

Super AC Subcontractor completed as much work as they possibly could but were eventually forced to abandon the project because they couldn't afford to pay for the work. As soon as Super AC Subcontractor left the project, the general contractor declared them in default and filed on their bonds. The surety paid the amounts demanded by the general contractor.

This is a true story, and it gets worse. Not only did the subcontractor go out of business, but all of the owner's personal assets were seized to repay the surety (the company that issued the bonds) that paid the claim.

"How?" you might be asking. Let me explain.

WHAT'S A SUBCONTRACTOR BOND?

The subcontractor bond is sold as a way for the general contractor to protect itself from the risk of the subcontractor going out of business, being unable to finish its scope of work, or pay its laborers and/or material suppliers. In the unfortunate case that it is used as a shield, it does not sound so bad. The bond works as a shield and protects the general contractor from the unfortunate event of a subcontractor going out of business or anything that would keep the subcontractor from performing. However, the bond could be used as a sword when the general contractor knows you have underbid the project and knows you cannot complete the work. They will then make you get a bond so they can file on the bond and make money off your tragic loss, as in the case of Super AC Subcontractor.

It's important to note that a subcontractor bond is *not insurance*. If there is a claim filed on your bond and the bond company pays the claim, you are required to pay back every penny that the surety pays out. To obtain a bond, you have to sign a personal guarantee and pledge your personal assets (more on this in chapter 5).

There are two different types of bonds: a payment bond and a performance bond. A payment bond is to ensure that all of your laborers and material suppliers are paid. If a general contractor receives a notice of claim from your laborers and/or material suppliers that they remain unpaid, the general contractor can file a claim on your bond for payment of those amounts. A performance bond will cover the cost to complete your scope of work if you abandon or are terminated from the project. If you do not finish your scope of work, the general contractor can file on your performance bond to seek the cost required to complete your scope. Normally, each bond is required to be in the full amount of your subcontract.

The paperwork required to be signed to obtain a bond is onerous, to say the least. Sureties require a personal guarantee from all of the principals of the company and a pledge of their personal assets and personal bank accounts to satisfy any amount paid by the surety.

Your agreement with the surety also gives them the sole discretion of whether to pay or deny a claim that is filed against your bond. What does this mean? For example, say a general contractor is trying to back charge you $200,000. You disagree with the requested back charge and explain to the general contractor why you disagree. Ignoring your argument, the general contractor files a claim on your bond for the $200,000. The bond company receives the claim and, without any input from you, pays the claim. In the paperwork you signed to get the bonds, you gave the surety the authority to decide to pay the claim. Now they are demanding you repay the $200,000 immediately, or they will begin collection efforts.

If you decide to take the risk and have a subcontractor bond issued, get to know the bond company and have them get to know and understand your company. If you establish a solid relationship with them, they are less likely to immediately pay a claim that is filed on your bond without hearing your side of the story. If you get a notice that a general contractor has filed a claim on your bond, you need to respond with your side of the story immediately, or the bond company will most likely just pay the claim.

HOW TO PROTECT YOUR COMPANY

If you are required to obtain a subcontractor bond, there are a few ways to protect your company, one of which is to add some language to your subcontract. The language in a subcontract requiring bonds is usually short and simple. For example:

> *Subcontractor shall provide performance and payment bonds if required by Contractor, on a form acceptable to Contractor, and by a surety acceptable to Contractor for the full amount of the subcontract.*

Or it might look something like this:

> *In the event that the Subcontract Agreement exceeds $100,000.00, Subcontractor shall furnish to the Contractor at Subcontractor's expense, surety bonds guaranteeing the faithful performance of this Subcontract Agreement and payment of all labors and material suppliers.*

The language as written is fine; it is what is missing that becomes harmful. First, you should not be required to provide a bond if you have already started working. Next, you need to add in some language that gives you some control over when your bond will pay claims. Finally, the cost of the bonds needs to be added to your subcontract amount.

Here is the language you would add to the paragraphs above to protect your company:

> *If Contractor does not request Subcontractor to provide a bond before Subcontractor begins work, Contractor waives its right to require Subcontractor to obtain a bond. If Contractor requests Subcontractor to obtain a bond, Contractor will reimburse Subcontractor for this expense. Subcontractor reserves the right to object to any claims filed on its bonds, and once Subcontractor objects, the surety shall not pay the claim until ordered by a court or arbitrator to do so.*

Another way to protect your company if you are required to obtain a subcontractor bond is to request a copy of the general contractor's bond. This way, if you cannot pay your laborers or material suppliers because the general contractor has not paid you, you can file on their bond.

There are no legal requirements for subcontractor bonds, which means that you can refuse to get a subcontractor bond and remove the provision requiring a bond from the subcontract before you sign. You may not get the project if you refuse, but now you know the risk and can make an informed decision.

When a general contractor requires their subcontractors to obtain bonds, it is referred to as "bonding back." Bonding back is the general contractor's way of mitigating their risk, because they are taking a risk in hiring your company. But what happens when the reason you cannot pay your bills for the project is because the general contractor is not paying you? You can file on the general contractor's bond for payment—but only if you have a copy of their bond.

It is best practice to get a copy of the general contactor's bond at the beginning of the project because the only way you can obtain a copy is from the general contractor. You can imagine how easy it would be to get a copy if you are not getting along.

SUBCONTRACTOR BONDS CAN BE DANGEROUS

I may be a little bit jaded on subcontractor bonds, but that's because I have never dealt with a successful subcontractor bond project. In fact, I have another client story to illustrate the danger of subcontractor bonds.

I represented a drywall subcontractor who was awarded a $300,000 contract for a public project that required special badges to access the project. Although the subcontract said that bonds could be required, none were required at the start of the project. About halfway through the project, the general contractor requested that my client obtain bonds. As required by the subcontract, my client complied and had a bond issued in the full subcontract amount. Because the subcontract did not have language preventing the general contractor from demanding a bond during the course of the project, my client had no choice but to comply or be in breach of the subcontract.

A few months later, when the subcontractor showed up for work one morning, the project manager stopped him at the entrance, demanded to see his access badge, and said they were no longer allowed on the project. Confused, my client immediately sent an email to the project manager and the higher-ups at the general contractor's office, asking what was going on and why his company's badges were pulled. In the email, he also stated that he was ready and able to perform the work, but he never received a response.

Five days later, my client received a notice of default letter for not performing his work on time. This same letter was sent to my client's bond company. My client promptly responded to the notice of default letter, explaining what had happened and attached an updated schedule to finish the project. My client sent this letter to the project manager, the higher-ups at the general contractor's office, and his bond company. Still, no response.

Fifteen days later, still being denied access to the project, my client received a notice of termination letter from the general contractor. My client was terminated for failing to perform his work promptly, and an official claim was filed on his bond. Fortunately, this particular bond company reviewed my client's response and did not pay the claim.

It certainly didn't look like this happened because of my client's poor performance. Instead, what most likely happened was the general contractor ran into money problems and thought of a creative way to make some of it back. Although my client was halfway through the project, the general contractor demanded that my client obtain a bond for the full contract amount. Because my client had a provision saying a bond may be required, but did not have specific language limiting *when* the bond could be required (like the suggestion above), my client was forced to obtain one or be in violation of the subcontract. After the bond was successfully acquired, my client was then locked out of the project, keeping him and his team from performing their work, which put them in default. Once in default, the general contractor filed on my client's bond.

In the general contractor's past experience, once they filed a claim on a subcontractor's bond, the bond company would just pay the claim. In this case, however, since my client had a relationship with the bond company and because he immediately responded in writing to the claim, instead of paying, the bond company began an investigation. This infuriated the general contractor, who immediately filed suit against the bond company, demanding payment of the claim.

The general contractor sued the bond company for $200,000, which they claimed as damages they suffered because my client failed to complete the project. That number was ridiculous—in fact, the whole lawsuit was ridiculous. Unfortunately, my client did not have the hundreds of thousands of dollars required to defend himself and prove his side of the story. Even if he could prove that he were wrongfully terminated, the subcontract had a termination for convenience clause, which meant they could terminate my client for no reason. (We will go over this clause in chapter 18.) My client couldn't just ignore the lawsuit either, because the bond company would pay the claim and then come after him and the four other family members who ran the company and had signed personal guarantees to get the bond. So we made the best deal we could. To prevent a huge judgment being taken against him, he agreed to pay the general contractor $50,000 in payments over two years.

This case still pisses me off because I could not do anything to fix it. But now you know how dangerous subcontractor bonds can be. This is why I want you to understand what is in your subcontract and learn what terms need to be negotiated. Quit just signing the subcontract without reading it just to get the work; it is not worth the risk. You risk all of your business and personal assets to obtain a subcontractor bond. If you decide the project is worth the risk of obtaining a bond, at least negotiate some protection in the subcontract.

Although we already touched on this a bit in chapter 1, in the next chapter, we will do a deep dive into what you should pay attention to when it comes to part of the subcontract called "Scope of Work."

KEY POINTS

- When you get a subcontractor bond, you are pledging your personal assets for the project.
- Build some protections into the subcontract, do not get a bond after you have started the project, and limit when the bond can pay out.
- If you get a bond for the project, make sure you get a copy of the general contractor's bond before you begin work.

CHAPTER 4

SCOPE OF WORK

"They can't deduct $23,000 from what they owe me for lintels; I never agreed to provide the lintels," Jeff said in a panic. "Structural steel subcontractors never provide the lintels; the masonry subcontractor would provide those."

Jeff owns Super Structural Steel Fabrication & Erection Subcontractor. He has been in the structural steel fabrication and erection business for more than twenty years and has never been required to provide lintels on a project.

"I did not put in my bid that I would do the lintels," Jeff quickly explained.

Unfortunately, I informed him that it did not matter what was in his bid—it only mattered what was in the scope attached to the subcontract that he signed.

After a close review of the documents, I found what happened. Although the lintels were not in his scope when Jeff bid the project, upon reviewing the sections of the specifications that were in the subcontract he signed, it stated that he must provide the lintels. From the time Jeff had bid the project to the time he signed the subcontract, the specifications had changed. Now the "metal fabrications" section said he was required to provide the loose lintels.

There was no defense to the $23,000 back charge; Jeff had to pay up.

WHAT IS THE SCOPE?

The scope is the description of the work that you are hired to do on a project. Multiple documents describe your scope of work. Most importantly, the scope is described in the plans and specifications. We have already addressed in chapter 2 the importance of a close review of these documents when you are bidding the project. Unfortunately, when you receive a subcontract from the general contractor, your bid is not included anywhere in the subcontract or in related documents. That means your bid is not used to describe your scope of work. Like I mentioned in chapter 1, the scope of work attached to the subcontract you receive in response to your bid could be completely different from your bid.

Now, you could try to include your bid as one of the sub-contract documents if you wanted to. To do this, you would add a reference to your bid in the list of subcontract documents. To take an example from chapter 2, it would look something like this:

Article 1 the Subcontract Documents

*The subcontract documents consist of (1) this Subcontract Agreement; (2) the Prime Contract (the contract between the owner and General Contractor); (3) the Plans and specifications dated 12-1-2019; (4) Modifications issued subsequent to the Prime Contract, whether before or after the execution of this Agreement; (5) Modification to the subcontract; and **(6) the proposal Subcontractor provided to General Contractor dated 1-1-2020.***

Number 6 was added, which now says that your bid/proposal is part of the subcontract. Just make sure number 6 lists some way to identify the bid/proposal—the date works well to do this.

This may not win the scope argument if there is a conflict between the scope and your bid, but it would put you in a better position to argue what you were actually hired to do.

Another problematic provision I have recently been finding in subcontracts when the scope is being defined is this:

All Work described in the subcontract documents and any other Work that could be reasonably inferred therefrom.

You need to remove this whole sentence from the subcontract before you sign it. This is an open checkbook for the general contractor to add any amount of work to your scope and say that you are not entitled to a change order for the additional work because you agreed to it. The key words to look for are "reasonably inferred." If you have a written agreement, nothing should have to be "reasonably inferred."

UNDERSTANDING THE SCOPE IS VITAL

The scope is by far the most important part of a subcontract. Agreeing to a scope that you have not reviewed could cost you and your company.

Once you sign, whatever is included in your scope and attached to the subcontract is what you will be required to do, whether or not the amount of the subcontract is enough to pay for the cost of all your work. If it is included in the scope of the subcontract you signed, you will not be given a change order for what you are required to do that was not in your bid.

Review the scope attached to the subcontract as if you are bidding a new project. Then compare the bid you did the first time with the scope attached to the subcontract. If the numbers are not the same, figure out why. If there was something added to your scope, send the general contractor a detailed letter explaining the difference and giving them the updated price. Then ask the general contractor to reissue the proposed subcontract with the new price.

Once the subcontract is reissued in the correct amount, then it is safe to sign. Do not start work until you receive and sign the updated contract. Do not rely on a statement that it will be added to the subcontract amount later either. That is unacceptable. Once you sign the contract, you will be held responsible to do the work described in the scope for the price in the subcontract, so be sure that it is accurate and that you and your company can afford it.

It is also important to make sure your scope is specific enough to protect your company. I represented Super Land Clearing Subcontractor, which was hired to remove dirt from a project site. When they began to work on the project, the city informed them that the dirt could not be hauled to just any dump site; it had to go to a permitted dump site. This substantially increased the cost of Super Land Clearing Sub's work. When they submitted a request for a change order to the general contractor for the increased cost, the request was denied. The general contractor said that their subcontract stated that Sub would remove the dirt and was not entitled to more money if it turned out to cost more. Super Land Clearing Sub's scope stated they were responsible for removing the dirt, but they should have been more detailed and included that the removal was only to a standard dump site and that if a permitted dump site was required, there would be additional cost. Not having that specific language cost Sub an extra $10,000 to remove the dirt to a permitted site.

What happens if you agree to a scope that is much larger than the subcontract amount? If possible, you must complete the scope of work you agreed to do, even if it means you will lose money. If you don't complete the work, you will not get paid for the work you have already completed. Additionally, the general contractor is entitled to collect from you any funds they pay over your subcontract amount to complete your work if you were unable to finish.

That is why understanding the scope attached to your subcontract is so important. Whatever scope is attached is the work you will be required to do, regardless of the cost.

Don't be like Jeff or Super Land Clearing Sub. Read and understand the scope, as it can be wildly different than your original bid. And just because your company may not offer a certain service, don't assume that it could not be in your scope. Something that is considered "industry standard" will not be a defense to an express subcontract provision that says the opposite.

You cannot use any other document or statement to interpret or explain the subcontract you sign, so be sure to give the scope of work the attention it deserves.

In the next chapter, we'll discuss how you should never sign a personal guarantee, which could destroy not only your business but your personal life as well.

KEY POINTS

- The scope is by far the most important part of a subcontract.
- The scope is the work you agree to do and is explained by the documents described in the subcontract.
- Your bid is not part of the scope.
- Review the scope attached to the subcontract as if you were bidding a new project, and make sure it matches your original bid.

CHAPTER 5

DO NOT SIGN A PERSONAL GUARANTEE

"How could they get my personal bank account?" Kelly from Super Electrical Subcontractor asked me desperately.

She was checking out at a grocery store when her card was declined. After she embarrassedly left the grocery store, she called her bank to find out what was going on. She knew she had plenty of money in that account. The only thing her bank could tell her was that all of her accounts had been garnished (frozen) by Sunset General Contractors.

Kelly recognized the name—a company she had only done business with once about a year ago. In fact, they still owed her money for that project. She called me in a panic to figure out what was going on. After some research, I discovered that Super Electrical Subcontractor and Kelly individually were sued by Sunset General Contractor. Kelly had never received notice of the lawsuit because it was served through her address listed on the Texas Secretary of State, which was an old address. If you do not answer a lawsuit, even if you are unaware of it, a judgment can still be taken against you. Sunset General Contractor was able to get a judgment against Kelly individually, even though she should have been protected from any liability of Super Electrical Subcontractor because it was a company. Kelly had signed a personal guarantee as part of her subcontract and agreed to be personally liable for the debts of her company.

WHAT'S A PERSONAL GUARANTEE?

Signing a personal guarantee means that if your business becomes unable to repay any debt, you as an individual assume personal responsibility for the balance. That means judgments can be made against your personal bank accounts and assets, like we saw with Kelly.

In my experience, a general contractor that asks you to sign a personal guarantee as part of a subcontract is "sucker fishing," meaning they do not actually expect you to sign it. They expect you either to say that you will not sign it or to send the subcontract back and sign everything but the personal guarantee. If you do sign the personal guarantee, however, it's a win for them. They will gladly accept it and use it against you.

The initial subcontract that the general contractor sends over is just their first offer. If you agree to everything, it's like paying the sticker price for a new car. Everyone knows the dealer will take less than the sticker price, and they expect you to negotiate. It's the same with a subcontract. The general contractor expects negotiations; it shows that you are informed and paying attention.

Although slightly different, subcontractor bonds (which we covered in chapter 3) are another form of personally guaranteeing your performance of a subcontract. When you sign personal guarantee paperwork with a bond company, the bond company then issues the general contractor a guarantee that you will complete the contract and pay everyone you hire. If you fail to perform, the bond company will pay the claim and then come after you for reimbursement. Unlike the personal guarantee that you sign in a subcontract, if the general contractor wants to recover funds from you personally, they have to sue you, and if you don't have the funds or you file bankruptcy, they will not get any money. The bond gives the general contractor faster and guaranteed payment if you default.

Being incorporated means you have filed paperwork with the Texas Secretary of State and your company is legally recognized as one of the following entities: a corporation, a limited liability company, a limited liability partnership, a limited partnership, or a professional corporation.

Which type of entity you choose will depend on the tax liability and the purpose of your business. Once you are incorporated, your business becomes its own entity and will need its own bank account that only business funds run through. You will become an employee of your company. It is vitally important that you keep the company's business separate from your individual income and expenses. If you do not treat your company as a separate entity, the law won't either. Using your company assets and accounts for personal expenses could lead to personal liability.

Make sure the address you have on file with the Secretary of State is up to date. Legal notices regarding your business will be sent to the address they have on file. You will be considered to have received such notices once they are sent to that address even if you don't actually receive the notice.

WHY YOU SHOULD INCORPORATE

Treating your company as its own entity is important

because of the protection it provides. Any debts or wrongdoing of the company can only be held against the company. For example, if your company signs a contract with an IT company for one year's worth of service, but after six months you switch companies, the first IT company can sue your company for the remaining six months left on the contract you canceled. Any lawsuit or resulting judgment would only be against the company, not you as an individual, meaning your personal accounts and assets will not be subject to collection of the IT company's judgment, but your company's assets would be.

When it comes to incorporating, there are a few important things to keep in mind.

Filing a DBA, which stands for Doing Business As, is *not* the same thing as incorporating. A DBA only describes a person doing business as a company name—for example, Josh Bacon DBA The Sprinkler Guys. A DBA provides no protection, even if you file an assumed name record with the county clerk. It is the same as just doing business individually.

If you sign a personal guarantee, you are waiving the protection you have because of your incorporated entity. You are agreeing to be personally liable for the debts of your company. You are agreeing that your personal assets will be available to satisfy the debts of your company.

I cannot repeat this enough: do not sign a personal guarantee as part of a subcontract.

Now, there are times when you have to sign a personal guarantee, like when you are buying property for your company, or if you are buying a vehicle or equipment for your business. In those circumstances, it is normal to sign a personal guarantee because you usually cannot negotiate the terms of a loan agreement with a bank for vehicles, equipment, or property. Do not, however, sign a personal guarantee as part of a subcontract; do not put up your personal assets in order to work on a construction project. Because it is not legally required, you can negotiate the terms of the subcontract to exclude the personal guarantee.

Whenever you sign any document on behalf of your incorporated company, make sure you sign your name and title in the company. For example, I always sign Karalynn Cromeens, Member, The Cromeens Law Firm, PLLC. When signing a company document with just your individual name, it can be argued that you signed in your personal capacity, and you are personally liable.

PROVISION LANGUAGE EXAMPLES

Here is one example of what a personal guarantee looks like:

AGREEMENT

In consideration of the Recitals, the covenants set forth herein and other good and valuable consideration the receipt and sufficiency of which are hereby acknowledged, and as an inducement to General Contractor to enter into the Agreement with Subcontractor, Guarantors hereby agree and acknowledge as follow:

Guarantors hereby unconditionally and irrevocably guarantee to General Contractor the due and punctual performance by Subcontractor of its obligation to fully and promptly pay all employees, agents, subcontractors, material supplier and labor suppliers of Subcontractor, to the same extent and effect as if Guarantors were the Subcontractor under the Agreement.

The parties comprising Guarantors shall have joint and several liabilities for the duties, liabilities, obligations and indebtedness of Guarantors under this Guarantee.

Guarantors agree to be bound by the provisions of the Agreement.

Here is another example:

I, _____ (name), residing at_____ (address)

Personally guarantee to you the payment of any obligation of the Company, and I hereby agree to bind myself to pay you on demand any sum, which may become due to you by the Company whenever the Company shall fail to pay the same. It is understood that this guaranty shall be a continuing and irrevocable guarantee and indemnity to such indebtedness of the Company. I do hereby waive notice of default, nonpayment and notice thereof and consent to any modification or renewal of the credit agreement hereby guaranteed.

Because Kelly wasn't aware of the lawsuit against her and thus didn't respond, her company Super Electrical Subcontractor was never able to collect the money they were initially owed by Sunset General Contractor. And because Kelly signed a personal guarantee, Sunset General Contractor successfully and legally collected its $5,000 judgment from her personal bank account. Even though Super Electrical Subcontractor was incorporated, when Kelly signed a personal guarantee as part of the subcontract, she waived the protections offered by incorporation and became personally liable for the debts of her company.

In the next chapter, I'll show you how to protect yourself from being responsible for the work from other subcontractors, and I'll explain why physically visiting a project site is a must.

KEY POINTS

- Do not sign a personal guarantee as part of a subcontract.
- If you are not incorporated, go get incorporated.
- Make sure you run your company as its own entity.
- When you sign a document for your company, make sure you use your name and title.
- If you sign a personal guarantee, you are waiving the protections offered through your incorporated entity.

CHAPTER 6

PRIOR WORK AND FIELD CONDITIONS

"Why did they sue me?" Linda from Super Paint Subcontractor asked me. "I'm the painting subcontractor; I had nothing to do with the issues with the drywall!"

Linda's company had been sued by a general contractor on a project they had already finished. The lawsuit claimed that there were substantial issues with the walls but said nothing about the paint being defective. Linda's company had only painted the walls; they did not install them. While I was reviewing the documents to prepare to answer the lawsuit, I found this statement in the subcontract agreement she had signed.

If any part of Subcontractor's Work depends upon the

Work of Contractor or another subcontractor, Subcon-tractor has the duty to inspect the Work of the previous subcontractor and report any defects to Contractor. Subcontractor's failure to report the defect makes them Subcontractor's defects as well, and Subcontractor is responsible for all damages related thereto.

This meant that since Linda did not find and report the drywall subcontractor's defaults to the general contractor, their defaults became her defaults. The whole deal ended up costing Linda $20,000—$10,000 for the attorney and $10,000 to the general contractor to settle the case, which is pretty ridiculous, considering there was nothing wrong with her work.

PRIOR WORK

It is essential to find this prior work language in your subcontract and remove or modify the provision. This is one of the reasons that all of the subcontractors on a project will be brought into a lawsuit, even when their scope of work was not found to be defective.

These dangerous provisions are in most subcontracts and deal with the work of the subcontractor before you. They often look something like this:

Before commencing work, Subcontractor will check the

Work performed by others and report in writing to the General Contractor any defect, interference, or non-conformity in the Work of others or in the plans and specification. Except to the extent Subcontractor reports defects, interferences, or non-conformities in writing, Subcontractor accepts the Work performed by others.

Here is another example:

If Subcontractor deems that surfaces of Work to which his Work is to be applied or affixed is unsatisfactory or unsuitable, written notification of said condition shall be given to the General Contractor before proceeding or taking remedial action. Otherwise, Subcontractor shall be fully and solely responsible and liable for any and all expense, loss, or damages resulting from said condition, and General Contractor shall be relieved of all liability in connection therewith.

This means that if the work of the subcontractor before you is messed up and you do not notice it and tell the general contractor about it in writing, you are now responsible to fix it. Or if you do not fix it, you are responsible for any damage the messed-up work may cause.

Are you kidding me?

If you have to catch the messed-up work of other subcontractors, then what exactly is the point of having a general contractor? Do not get me wrong—if you see something that another subcontractor messed up that the general contractor missed, you should say something, but you should not be financially responsible for the mess up of another subcontractor if you do not see the mistake.

This clause is the reason why, when the owner sues a general contractor for defects, the general contractor can sue all of the subcontractors on the project even if the defects the general contractor is sued for were not in the subcontractors' scope of work.

CHANGE THE LANGUAGE

This part of the subcontract should be changed. Below are some suggested clauses with language that do not put all the responsibility on you, the subcontractor.

> *Before commencing work, Subcontractor will check the Work performed by others and report in writing to the General Contractor any defect, interference, or non-conformity in the Work of others found by such inspection. Subcontractor will not be responsible for any non-conformities not reported.*

This clause is a fair requirement; it says you are required to do an inspection and report any nonconforming work that you find. You are not responsible, however, to fix any work, and you are not responsible if you happen to miss any nonconforming work.

Here is another example:

> *If Subcontractor deems that surfaces of Work to which their Work is to be applied or affixed is unsatisfactory or unsuitable, written notification of said condition shall be given to the General Contractor before proceeding or taking remedial action. Subcontractor will not be responsible for any unsatisfactory or unsuitable surfaces that are not reported.*

Again, we made this provision reasonable by removing the part where you become liable for the work of a previous subcontractor, but we kept in the duty to inspect before you perform your work.

The clauses about being responsible for a prior subcontractor's work can come in all different languages. You need to read the subcontract to find it and suggest a provision that is more reasonable before you sign the subcontract.

FIELD CONDITIONS

Most subcontracts have a provision dealing with the field conditions; they normally look something like this:

> *The Subcontractor hereby acknowledges and certifies it has visually examined the Work site and agrees that it is aware of all relevant site conditions, and everything regarding the site conditions is included in the contract price.*

Here is another example:

> *Subcontractor has conducted an inspection of the project site and is fully aware of the site and how it relates it the Subcontractor's scope of work.*

So, what exactly are they trying to get at with these provisions? If there is anything involving the site conditions that could increase your contract price, you will not be able to request additional funds to cover the increased price. This is why it is important to visit the project site before you sign the subcontract. Some things to take into consideration when you visit the project, make note of the following:

- **Parking:** Where can you park? Is parking free, or will you have to pay? What will you do if no parking is available? Taking an Uber to the project site every day can get expensive.

- **Restroom:** Is there a restroom on-site? Is a portable toilet being provided? Will you have to provide one?
- **Mobilization:** Is there something about the project site or where it is located that may increase your mobilization cost?
- **Deliveries/Storage:** Is there easy access to deliver materials? Is there a place to store materials on-site, or will you have to provide storage?
- **Safety Gear:** What kind of safety gear will you need? Is there something that you will need to purchase?

Visiting the project site before you sign the subcontract will ensure that you have considered all of these potential issues and that they are included in the contract price so that you will not lose money on the project.

Two other ways to prevent potential issues on a project are through submittal and as-built drawings, which we will cover in the next chapter.

KEY POINTS

- Find and change or remove the provision that makes your company responsible for the work of the subcontractors before you.
- Visit the project site before you sign the subcontract.

CHAPTER 7

SUBMITTALS
AND AS BUILTS

The judge read the jury's verdict, a judgment against my client, Super Door Subcontractor, for $150,000. All I could think was if my client had had something in writing approving the doors they installed, none of this would have happened.

Before Susan with Super Door Subcontractor began work on this particular project, the general contractor told them the owner wanted different doors than what was called for in the plans. Susan told the general contractor that the new doors the owner wanted would not work. The doors the owner wanted were designed for interior use and would not work for the exterior of the building where they were to be installed. The general contractor said the owner didn't care, and they wanted these doors.

Despite her hesitation, Susan did what the owner wanted and installed the doors the owner requested. When the doors failed, like she said they would, Susan was sued. Unfortunately, my client did not have any evidence, other than her word, that they were specifically instructed to install the doors that failed.

Had Susan had an approved submittal or proof that she sent over as-built drawings with a transmittal letter, as suggested in this chapter, this may not have happed.

If there was a way to CYA (cover your ass) from a dispute that may occur after the project is complete while the project was ongoing, would you do it?

That is what the submittal and as-built process can do for you—it can CYA!

THE SUBMITTAL PROCESS

A submittal is a process for getting the general contractor and/or owner to approve materials for a project before they are installed.

The submittal process, if done correctly, is a paper trail

that will prove that your work was approved by the general contractor and/or owner before you performed the work. As long as you do the work as it was presented in the submittal, the general contractor and/or owner cannot later refuse to pay you based on nonconforming work.

Not taking advantage of the submittal process is the loss of a valuable tool to document the acceptance of your work during the project.

Having the general contractor sign off on a submittal and/or a set of as-built drawings can potentially limit your liability if the general contractor later claims that your work was defective or that the materials you used were inadequate.

Most subcontracts have a provision that requires a submittal process. Meaning, material that is going to be supplied for the project must be approved before it is installed. Carpet, paint, windows, and stone should all be approved via submittal before the order for the material for the project is placed.

The submittal process is the process of gathering all of the documents that explain and describe the material and submitting that information to the general contractor and any other required parties. The submittal package includes all of the required documents with the required submittal form attached. All subcontractors that are required to supply material for a project should provide a submittal package to the general contractor and/or owner that includes the product data sheet for each product you plan to use and a sample of the actual material that will be used.

If allowed, request to do a mock-up, meaning you do a small application of the product on-site. This allows the general contractor and/or owner to see what the actual product looks like at the project site and allows a chance to change it if it is not what the owner was envisioning.

Some examples of the submittal process as written in subcontracts might look like this:

> *Subcontractor will prepare and submit to General Contractor, in a timely manner, all shop drawings, product samples, test results, installer's instructions, product data sheets, and any other relevant information, within 30 days of signing this subcontract. Subcontractor shall not begin any Work until the submittal package is approved.*

This particular subcontract did not have a specified submittal form that could be used. Visit **Subcontractor Institute.com** to download a submittal form that I suggest you use. The important part is keeping a copy of the signed approval.

Here is another example:

> *SHOP DRAWING AND SAMPLES: Subcontractor shall furnish promptly all samples, product data sheets, drawings, schedules, and shop drawings, as required in connection with Subcontractor's work. Approval of the submittal package does not relieve Subcontractor of the responsibility of complying with the drawings, specifications, and all contract documents.*

Although this paragraph states that the subcontractor still has the responsibility to comply with the drawings, specifications, and contract documents, the general contractor's approval of your work before you begin will be very convincing evidence that your work was accepted as is.

Ensure that the product you submit is in accordance with the specifications for the project and that the way it is applied or installed follows the manufacturers' guidelines. Failure to do so may void any warranty claims. Most suppliers and manufacturers will have the information that is required for a submittal package.

Another important aspect of the submittal process is

keeping a copy of all the documents submitted and the submittal form that is signed and accepted. Include in your submittal package an extra copy of everything that you have submitted with the submittal approval form. If a specific form is not required by your subcontract, you can find a form at **SubcontractorInstitute.com**. Make sure you do not move forward with the application and/or install until you have the signed submittal approval form.

Visit **SubcontractorInstitute.com** and download the "submittal acceptance form." From here on out, be sure to put your letterhead on every submittal you do. Make sure you get the signed approval back before you begin the application and/or installation. Save the signed form digitally and physically in your records for the project. If you do not keep a copy of your approved submittal, you will not be able to demonstrate that it was approved if there is an issue later on.

If Super Door Subcontractor had a signed submittal form approving the doors they installed, they would not have been sued or received a $150,000 judgment against them.

WHAT ARE AS BUILT DRAWINGS?

As-built drawings show how your scope was built, which is always slightly different than the proposed drawings. These documents are very important. It is easier and more effective to take notes and prepare these documents when you are on the project site as opposed to trying to remember what you did when the general contractor is demanding the as-built drawings to issue your last payment, or retainage.

Your as built drawings will be a part of the general contractor's closeout documents to the owner. A correct set of as built drawings are essential to the owner and their facilities team. A set of as built drawings will be required before you are issued final payment. In addition, if your information is included, the owner will be more likely to contact you if they want to upgrade or remodel.

To have effective as built drawings, you should make a note of any changes to your shop drawings, or anything else that was in the submittal package, that were applied and/or installed differently than what was initially submitted. Make the changes to the submittal documents the same day you become aware of the change. That way, when you complete your scope of work, you can send the general contractor/owner your as-built drawings instead of them being demanded from you. That way, you don't have to try to remember what happened at the project site and throwing something together at the last minute.

From a legal perspective, it will be more difficult for the general contractor and/or owner to claim that your work was not accepted when you send over the as built drawings as soon as your scope is completed. At **SubcontractorInstitute.com**, you will find a transmittal letter to attach to your as-built drawings when submitting them to the general contractor/owner. This letter will put the responsibility on the general contractor/owner to raise any issues with your work at that point in time, or they are waived.

Download the as-built drawings transmittal letter and make it part of your process to send the as-built drawings as soon as you complete your scope of work with the transmittal letter.

If you aren't already preparing and submittals and as-built drawings as part of your process, you need to start doing so immediately. Make sure you keep the signed approval of the submittal and/or as-built drawings as part of your project file. These should be some of the first documents you provide if a dispute arises.

In the next chapter, we'll discuss another important topic that you should be doing if you're not already: daily reports.

KEY POINTS

- Supply a submittal package to the general contractor even if it is not required by your subcontract.
- Get signed approval of your submittal package before you begin work.
- When your scope is complete, send the general contractor the as-built drawings along with the transmittal letter.

CHAPTER 8

———

DAILY REPORTS

"That is a lie," Chris from Super Everything Subcontractor whispered to me while in trial.

Chris's company had been sued for more than $700,000 for the cost to complete a project they were forced to abandon. The project manager was testifying on how Chris's company had failed to comply with the subcontract because they never turned in any daily reports.

"I did turn in daily reports, but I didn't keep a copy of what I turned in," Chris told me.

No one ever plans to get in a dispute with their general contractor or, even worse, to be sued by them. Having your side of the story written in daily reports, before there was ever an issue, is amazing evidence to have if you ever find yourself in such a situation. Spending the time filling them out daily—and making sure you keep a copy for yourself—is definitely worth it.

One of the most important things about a subcontract (or any contract in general, for that matter) is you do not want to breach it. You especially do not want to be the first to breach it. A breach in the contract is the failure to do one of the things that you agreed you would do in the contract. One of the things you agree to do in a subcontract is to fill out a daily report. The subcontract provisions that require a daily report normally look something like this:

> *Subcontractor will submit daily work reports to General Contractor, using the "Daily Report" form attached to this Subcontract.*

Or they may look something like this:

> *Subcontractor is required to submit and have an on-site project manager sign daily progress reports. Such reports can be submitted via email or hand delivery at the end of every day.*

The daily report describes what went on within the project and also acts as a way to voice any concerns with the project. This is a great tool for both the subcontractor and the general contractor. For the subcontractor, it creates a detailed timeline of the project. The subcontractor can also raise issues that they see at the project, whether it is related to their scope or not.

The daily report normally includes the following information:

- The project name and address
- The date
- A minor weather report
- The names of the people who were working on the project that day and the number of hours each person worked
- A record of any of your materials delivered to the project on that date
- A log of the work you performed that day
- A section for notes and comments (This is where you would put in writing any concerns you have.)
- Any required change orders (If something arises at the project that will require a change order, it is a good idea to bring it up here, in this part of the report.)
- Pictures (A good daily report will also include pictures.)

If your subcontract requires daily reports to be submitted, and you do not submit them on time, you are in breach of the subcontract. Take the time to fill out a daily report every day. Also, make sure you keep a copy of the daily report you submit. If you have to turn it in at the end of the day, take a picture with your phone so that you have a copy.

Before you sign the subcontract, request a copy of the daily report form that the general contractor would like you to use. There are also a lot of apps and services that will let you fill out a daily report electronically. If you want to submit electronic daily reports, ask the general contractor if there is a certain service or app they would prefer you to use.

Even if the subcontract does not require a daily report, it is a good idea to complete one for your own records, to prove your side of the story. The daily report will also help reduce disagreements about the amount of work you have completed when you submit your payment application.

If you do not already have a daily report form, you can download one for free at **SubcontractorInstitute.com**. Feel free to add anything you think is necessary for your company.

I know it is a pain in the ass to do these reports every day, and it's a pain to make copies for yourself. But sitting at a counsel table in a trial when you are being sued for breach of contract due to failure to turn in daily reports or make copies of them is not how you want to learn about their value. Don't make the same mistake Chris did.

Up next: we're tackling pay when paid clauses and how you can change them to be fairer.

KEY POINTS

- Do a daily report even if one is not required by your subcontract.
- Keep copies of the daily reports you turn in.

CHAPTER 9

PAY WHEN PAID CLAUSES

Pop quiz: Who is in the best position to finance a construction project? If you answered, "The owner," you'd be right. While the owner normally obtains funds from a bank to pay for construction, they are not the ones who finance the project.

The subcontractors are the ones who end up financing the project.

That's right! Those who put out labor, material, and then wait to be paid are the ones financing the project. Those who have to make payroll every week regardless of whether the check from the general contractor shows up are the ones backing the project.

How is it possible for the companies with the least amount of resources to end up financing the project? Subcontractors are only paid after they perform their work. The owner and the general contractor receive the value of the subcontractor's work before they have to pay for it. How can this even happen?

Enter the pay when paid clause.

WHAT'S A PAY WHEN PAID CLAUSE?

The pay when paid clause means that the general contractor has no obligation to pay the subcontractor until the general contractor receives payment for the subcontractor's work from the owner.

In the not-so-distant past, when a general contractor hired a subcontractor, they promised to pay the subcontractor for their work. Now the general contractor promises to pay the subcontractor, but only after they are paid by the owner. Now the subcontractor is waiting for some event that they have no control over (the owner paying the general contractor) in order to get paid. Just performing the work in a good and workmanlike manner (the get-shit-done tribe!) is not enough to be paid these days.

Ensuring that you have submitted all the required documents with your pay application is only the first step to being paid on time. If there's a problematic pay when paid clause in your subcontract, it puts the fate of your timely payment outside of your control.

There are many things out of the subcontractor's control that can delay the payment from the owner. What if the general contractor does not timely submit its pay application? What if bad work performed by another subcontractor stops all payments from the owner to the general contractor?

The question then becomes, how long can you afford to go without pay for the work you already performed?

PROVISION LANGUAGE EXAMPLES

Below are some examples of pay when paid clauses and how to change them to negotiate a better position for your company. This way not all of the risk of nonpayment from the owner falls on you.

Here is language that you want to watch out for and replace:

General Contractor and Subcontractor agree that the owner's payment to General Contractor is an absolute condition precedent to General Contractor's obligation to pay Subcontractor any progress or final payment.

Subcontractor expressly agrees that it retains the risk of the owner's insolvency or inability to pay General Contractor.

Now here is how you should change the clause to give yourself some protection:

General Contractor and Subcontractor agree that the owner's payment to General Contractor is an absolute condition precedent to General Contractor's obligation to pay Subcontractor any progress or final payment. If the owner does not pay General Contractor within 30 days of receiving Subcontractor's pay application, and Subcontractor is not the reason the General Contractor is not being paid, the General Contractor will pay Subcontractor the amount due for that pay application by the 40th day after the pay application was submitted to the General Contractor.

Here is another problematic example you would want to replace:

The General Contractor shall pay the Subcontractor each progress payment within seven working days after the General Contractor receives payment from the owner. If the General Contractor does not receive payment from the owner, General Contractor has no obligation to pay the Subcontractor.

Here is some suggested language to make the provision a little fairer:

The General Contractor shall pay the Subcontractor each progress payment within seven working days after the General Contractor receives payment from the owner. If the owner fails to pay the General Contractor within 30 days of the General Contractor receiving Subcontractor's pay application, and Subcontractor is not the reason General Contractor is not being paid, the General Contractor will pay for Subcontractor to file its lien for the unpaid amount, up to $2,000.

Here is another ridiculous example:

Payment of General Contractor by owner for Subcontractor's Work is a condition precedent to General Contractor's obligation to pay Subcontractor. Subcontractor understands and acknowledges that Subcontractor relies on the credit of the owner, not the General Contractor, for payment of Subcontractor's work.

What this is saying is, the subcontractor is supposed to rely on the owner for payment! The subcontractor doesn't have a contract with them nor would they have the chance to examine their financial records to determine if they wanted to rely on their financial condition for payment of their work. I have an idea! What if the subcontractor approached the general contractor and said, "Why don't you get me the owner's financial information so I can make an informed decision?" Ha! The general contractor will never give you that information, which is why that sentence needs to be removed, along with some other changes. Here is a revision to the example above:

> *Payment of General Contractor by owner for Subcontractor's Work is a condition precedent to General Contractor's obligation to pay Subcontractor. If the owner does not pay the General Contractor within 30 days, of receiving Subcontractor's pay application, and Subcontractor is not the reason the General Contractor is not being paid, the General Contractor will pay Subcontractor 50% of the amount Subcontractor is owed for that pay application, and the remaining 50% will be paid once the General Contractor receives the funds from the owner.*

A WAY OUT

If you signed a subcontract that contains a pay when paid clause, not all hope is lost. There is a way out. If you have submitted a pay application, and it's been forty-five days, and you have not been paid, and you are not the reason the general contractor has not been paid, you can get out of the pay when paid clause.

Here is what you need to do: send a letter to the general contractor stating that you do not want the pay when paid clause to be enforced against you, and demand payment. That's it! I know it sounds kind of ridiculous, but it's true. I don't make the laws; I just learn them and pass the information on.

At **SubcontractorInstitute.com**, you can download the letter you need to send to the general contractor to stop the pay when paid clause from being enforced against you. It is called the Escape Clause Letter.

NEGOTIATE FOR YOURSELF

You should walk into every subcontract expecting to negotiate. You have to understand that the subcontract that is received for the project is only the first offer. This means it has everything the general contractor could want and more.

The general contractor does not expect you to agree to everything in the subcontract, but the general contractor will be accepted if you do. The general contractor expects you to negotiate the subcontract and is surprised and concerned when you do not.

In the next chapter, I'll encourage you to stop doing what you've always done by just signing a subcontract without negotiating.

KEY POINTS

- Pay when paid clauses make your timely payment condition upon an action you cannot control. The owner must pay the general contractor in order for you to be paid.
- You should not have to take all the risk of nonpayment from the owner. Negotiate pay when paid provisions.

CHAPTER 10

———

RETAINAGE

Every Christmas, my Auntie Karen would cut the ends off the ham before she put it in the oven.

"Why do you do that?" I asked her one year.

"I'm not sure, but my mom always did, so I do too."

Sometime later, Auntie Karen told me that her mom had cut off the ends of the ham because it would not fit in any of the pans that she owned, which was not a problem for my Auntie Karen. She cut the ends off because that is what her mother had always done.

This story reminds me of subcontractors' approaches to retainage. They do not know why they do it, but it has always been done a certain way, so that's what they'll continue to do.

However, it is crucial to understand what retainage is, because it will increase your leverage.

WHAT IS RETAINAGE?

Retainage is 10% of the contract amount between the owner and the general contractor on any project. Although the legal definition of retainage states nothing about subcontractors, most general contractors take 10% from the amounts due to the subcontractor throughout the project.

Retainage is important for a few reasons. First, it can limit the owner's liability if properly withheld. If the owner withholds 10% of the general contract amount from the general contractor until 30 days after completion, the owner's liability to lien claimants will only be the 10%. If the amount of the lien claimants exceeds the retainage amount, the valid lien claimants will share the 10% on a pro rata basis.

The owner's liability can be increased to an amount that is larger than the 10% if you trap the funds in the hands of the owner before the funds are paid to the general contractor. If you send an intent-to-lien letter that contains the required statutory statements, the funds due to the general contractor should be held in the hands of the owner until you are paid (download the letter at **SubcontractorInstitute.com**). If the owner pays any funds to the general contractor after they received such notice, the owner would be on the hook to pay again. Meaning the retainage amount would be increased by any payments the owner made after they received such notice. This means the sooner you send a notice of any unpaid amounts to the owner, the more likely you are to increase the owner's liability, and the more likely you will be paid the full amount you are owed.

Second, if the owner properly withholds the 10%, the period for filing liens can be shortened. If the project is completed, an affidavit of completion is filed with the county clerk, and the owner withholds the 10%, all liens must be filed within thirty days of completion. Normally, a lien claimant has until the fifteenth day of the fourth calendar month (around 120 days) after the last material was supplied to the project. This period can be shortened to thirty days after completion, regardless of when your work is performed, if the owner withholds retainage for thirty days after final completion.

Retainage generally does not become due to the subcontractor until thirty days after completion and/or when the general contractor receives the retainage payment.

To ensure that a subcontractor will have a valid lien on retainage, they should file their liens within thirty days of the project being completed.

What does this mean in the real world? Let's illustrate it through an example. If a general contract to build a shopping center was set at $1 million, retainage would be $100,000. Let's say that at the end of the project, the general contractor did not pay anyone out of the last payment request. All of the subcontractors were smart and filed their liens in a timely manner, and all of those lien claims totaled $300,000. But say the owner held the retainage until thirty days after the project was complete. In that case, the owner will only have to pay those lien holders $100,000, meaning the subcontractors will have to share pro rata, based on the amount they are owed. The larger the claim, the more they will receive. Even though they all have valid liens, they will not be paid in full.

Now, if one of those lien claimants had sent a notice *before* the owner had paid the general contractor the last draw, they would have been able to increase the amount they receive by the amount the owner paid the general contractor in that last draw. As a subcontractor, you never know when the owner will pay the general contractor, so the sooner you send your notice, the more likely you will be able to trap funds in the owner's hands. There is no penalty for sending notice of unpaid amounts early, but it will invalidate your lien if you send them late.

Doing things a certain way, just because they have always been done that way and you really don't know why, can lead to absurd results. Like cutting the end off of a perfectly good ham, or having 10% taken out of the amount you are owed, and not really knowing why. Another issue where I notice Subcontractors doing what they have always done without understanding why is when they do not file a lien when they are owed money. Don't worry. We will clear up all those misconceptions in the next chapter.

KEY POINTS

- Retainage can limit the owner's liability to 10% of the prime contract amount.
- File your lien for retainage when the project is complete to ensure that you will be paid retainage on time.

CHAPTER 11

WHEN CAN I
FILE A LIEN?

"I signed a subcontract that said I could not file a lien, but you're telling me I could have filed a lien for the $50,000 I'm owed?" Shane from Super Duper Subcontractor asked me in dismay.

Shane had listened to promises from the general contractor that his payment was coming for the last ninety days, but he had still not received payment, and now the general contractor had filed for bankruptcy.

Shane came to me to see what his options were. I had news for him, but nothing good. Since Shane had not sent the required notices on time, he could not file a lien against the project because it would be invalid. He could file a claim on the general contractor's bankruptcy, but his chances of being paid anything were slim to none.

Do not be like Shane; know the steps you have to take to collect your money, and *never* let the promises of payment push you outside of your required notice dates.

YOU CAN ALWAYS FILE A LIEN

First, any provision in a subcontract that says you cannot file a lien is unenforceable. That means even if you sign a subcontract that states you cannot file a lien, you can still file a lien.

Let me explain why your lien rights are so very important. When you are working on a project and are owed money, without a lien, the only way you can collect is by suing the general contractor for breach of the subcontract for not paying you. That is an unsecured debt. When you owe a credit card company for the money you spent at Home Depot, for example, the only way they can collect their money is to put your file into collections and sue you.

On the other hand, with a lien, you have secured debt. When purchasing a house, for example, you borrow money from a bank, and if you do not pay the bank, they would kick you out of the house and sell it for the money you owed them. A lien works the same way. If you are not paid for labor and/

or materials supplied to a construction project and you properly file a lien, you can force the sale of the property to pay your lien. I must say that 99% of cases do not end up with the sale of the property, but the lien claims end up being paid—which is what you want. Because having a lien is such a powerful remedy, you must follow the proper process. I would love to get into the details here, but subcontractor collections is a topic for a whole other book.

Many deadlines must be met to file a proper lien, but there is no penalty for filing a lien early. Meaning if it becomes clear from the circumstances that you will not be paid, no matter what phase the project is in, do not wait; file your lien.

A lien gives you leverage. Any project that has construction financing has to move from construction financing to permanent financing. Before a project can go to permanent financing, all liens must be taken care of. Even if the project is already in permanent financing, your lien will still have leverage. No owner wants a lien on their property, and they will pressure the general contractor to take care of any liens. Owners especially don't like to get sued for foreclosure of a lien that is against their property.

Don't waive your lien rights by signing an unconditional lien waiver when you have not been paid. We will cover this and more in the next chapter.

KEY POINTS

- No subcontract can stop you from filing a lien.
- A lien secures the amount you are owed with the property.
- A lien gives you leverage.

CHAPTER 12

———

LIEN WAIVERS

"What do you mean I can't collect my money?" Brad from Super Masonry Subcontractor questioned.

Brad was owed $50,000 for work he had done on a dentist office. The general contractor told him to sign an unconditional lien waiver and then he would be paid. Brad signed the waiver but never received a check, so he hired me to file a lien.

I made some phone calls and sent the intent to lien letter, and almost immediately, I received a nasty letter from the general contractor's attorney stating that any lien that Super Masonry Subcontractor filed against the project would be fraudulent and that the company will be sued if I filed the lien. The only basis for the general contractor's claim that the lien would be fraudulent was, you guessed it, because Brad had signed the unconditional lien waiver. I could not successfully argue against it because it had the following statement at the top of the lien waiver:

> *This document waives rights unconditionally and states that you have been paid for giving up those rights. It is prohibited for a person to require you to sign this document if you have not been paid the payment amount set forth below. If you have not been paid, use a conditional release form.*

Subcontractors are asked to sign unconditional waivers without being paid all the time, and most of the time, there is no issue and you get paid what you are owed. My job is to warn you about what *could* happen. In my experience, if you have been working with a general contractor for a long time and you have always signed unconditional waivers before you are paid, it most likely will not be an issue. However, do not sign an unconditional lien waiver if you have not been paid by someone you're working with for the first time. The unconditional lien waiver will be used against you when you are not paid and try to take further action to collect your money. You waived your rights to collect your funds when you signed the unconditional lien waiver.

STANDARD FORMS IN TEXAS

Before the state came up with the standard forms, there used to be all kinds of unnecessary language in lien waivers. This changed in 2011 when the Texas legislature created a set of standard lien waiver forms to make everything uniform and clear. These lien waiver forms are to be used in the state of Texas for all construction projects. They are found at sections 53.281–53.287 of the Texas property code. Although these are Texas forms, they are standard and could be used in any state. To download these forms, visit **SubcontractorInstitute.com**.

The standard forms include the following:

- Conditional waiver and release on progress payment
- Unconditional waiver and release on progress payment
- Conditional waiver and release on final payment
- Unconditional waiver and release on final payment

HOW LIEN WAIVERS WORK

1. You submit a conditional waiver on progress payment with your payment application.
2. The general contractor pays you for that pay application (make sure the check clears the bank).
3. You give the general contractor an unconditional waiver and release on progress payment for the pay-

ment you received (easy if you submit it with your next pay application). This is how the process goes while the project is ongoing.

4. For your final pay application and bill for retainage, you submit a conditional waiver and release on the final payment that includes the amount you are owed for retainage.

5. Once you are paid for your final pay application and retainage, and once the check clears, you give the general contractor an unconditional waiver and release on final payment.

Here are the forms in order.

CONDITIONAL WAIVER AND RELEASE
ON PROGRESS PAYMENT

Project _____

Job No. _____

On receipt by the signer of this document of a check from
_____ (maker of check) in the sum of $_____
payable to _____ (payee or payees of check) and
when the check has been properly endorsed and has been paid by the
bank on which it is drawn, this document becomes effective to release
any mechanic's lien right, any right arising from a payment bond that
complies with a state or federal statute, any common law payment bond
right, any claim for payment, and any rights under any similar ordinance,
rule, or statute related to claim or payment rights for persons in the signer's position that the signer has on the property of _____
(owner) located at _____ (location) to the following extent: _____ (job description). This
release covers a progress payment for all labor, services, equipment, or
materials furnished to the property or to _____ (person
with whom signer contracted) as indicated in the attached statement(s)
or progress payment request(s), except for unpaid retention, pending
modifications and changes, or other items furnished.

Before any recipient of this document relies on this document, the recipient should verify evidence of payment to the signer.

The signer warrants that the signer has already paid or will use the funds received from this progress payment to promptly pay in full all of the signer's laborers, subcontractors, materialmen, and suppliers for all work, materials, equipment, or services provided for or to the above referenced project in regard to the attached statement(s) or progress payment request(s).

Date _____

_____ (Company name)

By _____ (Signature)

_____ (Title)

NOTICE:

This document waives rights unconditionally and states that you have been paid for giving up those rights. It is prohibited for a person to require you to sign this document if you have not been paid the payment amount set forth below. If you have not been paid, use a conditional release form.

UNCONDITIONAL WAIVER AND
RELEASE ON PROGRESS PAYMENT

Project _____

Job No. _____

The signer of this document has been paid and has received a progress payment in the sum of $_____ for all labor, services, equipment, or materials furnished to the property or to _____ (person with whom signer contracted) on the property of _____ (owner) located at _____ (location) to the following extent: _____ (job description). The signer therefore waives and releases any mechanic's lien right, any right arising from a payment bond that complies with a state or federal statute, any common law payment bond right, any claim for payment, and any rights under any similar ordinance, rule, or statute related to claim or payment rights for persons in the signer's position that the signer has on the above referenced project to the following extent:

This release covers a progress payment for all labor, services, equipment, or materials furnished to the property or to _____ (person with whom signer contracted) as indicated in the attached statement(s) or progress payment request(s), except for unpaid retention, pending modifications and changes, or other items furnished.

The signer warrants that the signer has already paid or will use the funds received from this progress payment to promptly pay in full all of the signer's laborers, subcontractors, materialmen, and suppliers for all work, materials, equipment, or services provided for or to the above referenced project in regard to the attached statement(s) or progress payment request(s).

Date _____

_____ (Company name)

By _____ (Signature)

_____ (Title)

CONDITIONAL WAIVER AND
RELEASE ON FINAL PAYMENT˙

Project _____

Job No. _____

On receipt by the signer of this document of a check from
_____ (maker of check) in the sum of $_____
payable to _____ (payee or payees of check) and
when the check has been properly endorsed and has been paid by the
bank on which it is drawn, this document becomes effective to release any
mechanic's lien right, any right arising from a payment bond that complies
with a state or federal statute, any common law payment bond right, any
claim for payment, and any rights under any similar ordinance, rule, or
statute related to claim or payment rights for persons in the signer's position that the signer has on the property of _____
(owner) located at _____ (location) to the following extent: _____ (job description).

This release covers the final payment to the signer for all labor, services, equipment, or materials furnished to the property or to
_____ (person with whom signer contracted).

Before any recipient of this document relies on this document, the recipient should verify evidence of payment to the signer. The signer warrants
that the signer has already paid or will use the funds received from this
final payment to promptly pay in full all of the signer's laborers, subcon-

tractors, materialmen, and suppliers for all work, materials, equipment, or services provided for or to the above referenced project up to the date of this waiver and release.

Date _____

_____ (Company name)

By _____ (Signature)

_____ (Title)

NOTICE:

This document waives rights unconditionally and states that you have been paid for giving up those rights. It is prohibited for a person to require you to sign this document if you have not been paid the payment amount set forth below. If you have not been paid, use a conditional release form.

UNCONDITIONAL WAIVER AND
RELEASE ON FINAL PAYMENT

Project _____

Job No. _____

The signer of this document has been paid in full for all labor, services, equipment, or materials furnished to the property or to _____ (person with whom signer contracted) on the property of _____(owner) located at _____(location) to the following extent: _____ (job description). The signer therefore waives and releases any mechanic's lien right, any right arising from a payment bond that complies with a state or federal statute, any common law payment bond right, any claim for payment, and any rights under any similar ordinance, rule, or statute related to claim or payment rights for persons in the signer's position.

The signer warrants that the signer has already paid or will use the funds received from this final payment to promptly pay in full all of the signer's laborers, subcontractors, materialmen, and suppliers for all work, materials, equipment, or services provided for or to the above referenced project up to the date of this waiver and release.

Date _____

_____ (Company name)

By _____ (Signature)

_____ (Title)

Under section 52.283 of the Texas property code, it is illegal to make anyone sign either type of unconditional lien waiver if they have not been paid. This, unfortunately, happens all the time. It is not likely that this law would save you if you do sign an unconditional lien waiver if you have not been paid.

If you sign an unconditional lien wavier and are not paid the amount that is in that lien waiver, you have waived your right to be paid that amount. All of the work that was represented in that lien waiver, you just did for free. If it is going to cost you to have a customer, they are not worth having. You are better off staying at home than paying your customer to work for them, which is what happens if you sign an unconditional lien waiver and are not paid.

Although the general contractor does have a legal obligation to pay you once they are paid, which we will cover in the next chapter, signing a lien waiver that says you have been paid when you have not will alleviate that obligation.

KEY POINTS

- Do not sign an unconditional lien waiver if you have not been paid.
- There are standard lien waiver forms; do not sign a waiver unless it is the standard form.

CHAPTER 13

TRUST FUNDS

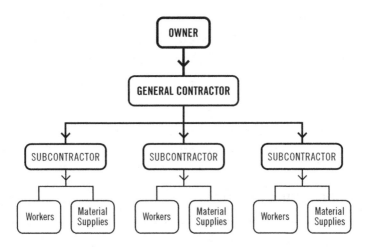

The money on a construction project has to move through many hands, so how can you be sure that everyone will be paid? Perfecting your lien rights is one way, but that is a whole other book.

The other way is through the law regarding trust funds.

WHAT IS A TRUST FUND?

The money received for a construction project is in the form of trust funds, which must be used to pay workers and material suppliers for the work they did on the project, not to buy a new car and fancy trips.

When an owner, general contractor, or subcontractor receives payment on a construction project and there are outstanding amounts due for labor or material on that project, those funds are considered held in trust for those workers and/or material suppliers. By law, those funds are considered trust funds. That means once you are paid on a project, you need to pay your bills for that project, or you are breaking the law. This also applies to the owner and general contractor.

You do not need to create a new bank account for each project (but you certainly can if it will help you keep everything in order). You do, however, need to easily trace the funds you receive on a construction project. Your records should show where the money came into your account and where that money was spent on that project. If you are hired by an individual homeowner to work on or to build a new house in an amount more than $5,000, then you are legally required to put those funds into their own construction account.

A WAY TO RECOVER FROM THE OWNER

Generally, as a subcontractor, you have no grounds to sue an owner directly. A properly filed lien is one way, but let's say you miss the timelines and cannot file a lien. In that case, you could sue the owner for a trust fund violation if you believe the owner spent the construction funds on things other than construction. If it can be proven that the owner misapplied the construction funds, the owner can be held personally responsible for the funds that were misapplied.

This also means that if *subcontractors* misapply construction funds, the company and the individual owners could be held liable for those funds.

Where many subcontractors go wrong is when something goes wrong on Project A, and they are not paid on time. However, they are paid on Project B, and instead of using the funds to pay the bills for Project B, they use the funds to pay for Project A. This is a misapplication of construction funds and is against the law—do not do it.

The best plan is to properly protect your lien rights on Project A. Let your material suppliers and workers know that you have not been paid on Project A so they can properly perfect their lien rights. Whether or not you are paid by the general contractor, you still have the obligation to pay your workers and material suppliers. Subcontractors and material suppliers appreciate your business and are willing to work with you through difficult projects, but you have to let them know what is going on so that they can protect their money too.

What happens if you use the funds from Project B to pay for Project A? The general contractor on Project B will have the right to pay your workers and material suppliers directly out of your funds when they get a notice that the worker and/or material suppliers have not been paid, causing a cash-flow crunch later on. You could also be sued for a trust fund violation. This would result in both your company and you individually being named in a lawsuit you would have to defend. Whoever is suing you would also have the right to subpoena all of your personal and company bank and credit card records. Even if you did not misapply the funds, they will be allowed to look through all of your records for themselves. This is a painful and expensive process.

Trust me, if you take a trip or show up in a new vehicle while working on a project, it will be noticed. I am not saying you cannot have or that you do not deserve nice things—you absolutely do—but make sure you pay your bills first. In the same turn, if you are not getting paid on a project, and the owner and/or general contractor shows up in a brand-new Land Rover or takes a week vacation to Paris, write it down. Note the dates it happened and what specifically caught your attention. If you are not paid, this information can be very important later on.

CRIMINAL CHARGES

A general contractor or subcontractor that misapplies construction trust funds could also face criminal charges for the funds that are misapplied. The charges range from a Class A misdemeanor to a felony of the third degree. It is a defense to a trust fund claim that you spent all of the funds that you received for a construction project on that project. Having the records to prove that you spent all of the funds on the project is essential. You must keep accurate records at all cost.

Another place where it is essential to maintain accurate and complete records is change orders, which we will cover in the next chapter.

KEY POINTS

- Everyone who receives funds on a construction project has the legal obligation to use those funds to pay everyone they owe money to for work on that project.
- Do not use funds from one project to pay for your debts on a different project. That is breaking the law.
- You could be personally liable for any misapplication of construction funds.
- Your personal and business accounts and credit card statements can be subpoenaed if you are sued for a trust fund violation.

CHAPTER 14

CHANGE ORDERS

Do you like to work for free? That is what you are doing when you complete extra work without a written change order. You are taking food from your family's table and giving it to someone else. Churches and charities are perfect places to give to others, but a business transaction is no place for charity.

"I was doing them a favor" are the first words I hear from most of my clients who end up in a legal dispute on a project. They had completed a few extra thousand dollars' worth of work at no charge to try to make their clients happy.

This kind of charity almost always ends in the subcontractor being sued and their clients demanding a refund.

Favors have their place, but it is not in any construction

projects. If you want to make your clients happy, show up when you say you will, take their phone calls, and answer their questions honestly, even if it is not what they want to hear.

WHAT IS A CHANGE ORDER?

The change order provision in a subcontract is what allows the parties to increase or decrease the subcontract price. An increase in the subcontract price is generally due to work being added to the scope and a decrease is generally due to work being removed from the scope.

All change orders should be in writing and be done in accordance with the subcontract provision that details the change order process. **If you do extra work without getting a signed change order, you will not be paid for the extra work.**

Even if you have to carry an invoice book that you purchased from Office Depot to record every time you are about to perform extra work, write it down with the price and get your client to sign off.

PROVISION LANGUAGE EXAMPLES

Every subcontract will have a provision dealing with change orders. Make sure you read and are familiar with the requirements to get a change order approved before you sign the subcontract. Below are a few examples of what a change order provision might look like:

Should General Contractor, at any time during the progress of the work, request any changes in the scope of the subcontract work. General Contractor shall have the right and power to make such a request. Subcontractor shall within five (5) days thereafter submit an itemized estimate reflecting any cost changes required to make the changes. It is distinctly understood and agreed, regardless from whom orders may be taken for changes in the scope of the subcontract work, that no such changes are to be made except by a subcontract change order issued by General Contractor and then only when such order sets forth the amount of any addition or deduction and is signed by both parties thereto. If Subcontractor initiates a substitution, deviation, or change in the work, which affects the Subcontract Work or causes expense to General Contractor, Subcontractor shall be liable for the expenses thereof.

It is your job to ensure that the technicalities of the subcontract provision are followed. For example, if under the following provision you submit the requested increase in price for a requested change order and do the work before the actual change order is signed by the general contractor, you will not be entitled to payment for the extra work.

Another important part of this provision is the last line, which says if you do the extra work without the signed change order, it will be your responsibility to pay for the extra work.

Here is another example:

> *In the event that the General Contractor directs Subcontractor to perform extra or additional work, Subcontractor will promptly perform and complete such Work whether or not General Contractor and Subcontractor have agreed on the cost of such work. Subcontractor shall submit a change order request within five (5) days of the requested work, or the claim for additional funds is waived. Subcontractor will only be entitled to the actual cost of the Extra Work and must submit proof of its actual cost with the change order request. Subcontractor acknowledges that General Contractor's field superintendents do not have authority to authorize Extra Work or to approve requested change orders; all requests for change orders must be sent to the following email address: Notgoingtobeapproved@ gmail.com.*

The first thing to notice and have addressed before you sign a subcontract with this change order provision is: Who is authorized to direct the subcontractor to perform extra work if it is not the filed superintendent?

The next thing to note is that if you do not submit the request for a change order within five days, you waive the right to payment for the extra work. In addition, I would try to negotiate that the subcontractor gets cost plus 5% (or whatever your normal profit margin is) for all extra work.

Below is an example of a fair change order provision that you could put into any subcontract.

Contractor may, at any time, direct Subcontractor to make changes, additions, and deletions concerning the Work. Any increase or decrease in the pricing of the Work resulting from such changes shall be agreed upon by the parties. If Subcontractor and Contractor cannot agree on the pricing of a change, then Subcontractor shall provide any cost information reasonably requested by Contractor. Subcontractor's provision of requested information is a condition precedent to payment. If no agreement on pricing is reached, Subcontractor shall be paid cost plus 15% for any additional work. If the requested change order increased Subcontractor's time to complete its scope of work, Subcontractor will be entitled to extra time, and such request must be listed on the change order.

REQUEST EXTRA TIME

If the work requested by the change order will make it impossible for you to complete your scope of work by the deadline you committed to in the project schedule, make sure you request extra time be added to your completion date in the change order. Don't assume that the general contractor should know it will take extra time. Make sure that if you are given extra time, it is in writing. A verbal agreement that you will be given extra time means nothing.

EXAMPLE CHANGE ORDER FORM

Download a change order request form at **Subcontractor Institute.com** that you can put your letterhead on and use if you do not already have one. It looks something like this:

(Insert your letterhead)

JOB NAME: _____

JOB ADDRESS: _____

CHANGE ORDER # _____

DATE: _____

OWNERS: _____

_____

_____

OWNERS hereby agree to the following changes in the plans and specifications of the project, and to the additional materials, supplies, services, labor, and other items listed below that are required to complete this Change Order. All other terms and conditions in the contract with _____ (your company name) shall remain the same...

CHANGES IN WORK (describe extra work):

_____

_____

_____

Charge Order Amount $ _____

AMOUNT OF ADDITIONAL TIME (the parties agree that some amount of time will be added to the currently set completion day; put down number of day to be added or new completion date)

_____

Payment for this Change Order is due upon completion of the change order work. All provisions of the contract between the above parties pertaining to the above job are applicable to this agreement. This Change Order may extend the time required to complete the project.

[Your business name here]

Accepted this _____ day of _____

By _____

By _____

OWNERS (Put name and address)

Accepted this _____ day of _____

By _____

By _____

GET PAID FOR YOUR WORK

This is business; make sure you are paid for all of the work you do, including the work that is added to your original scope of work. Read the change order provision in every subcontract before you sign it. If you do not understand, ask questions. It is not stupid to ask questions if you do not understand. It is stupid not to. Once you sign the subcontract, it will be too late.

Just like you expect to be paid when you are hired to do work, the owner/general subcontractor expects you to do the work they hired you to do and that you will not hire someone else to do it. Most subcontracts contain provisions against letting you sub out your work, which is what we will cover in the next chapter on assignments.

KEY POINTS

- If you don't get a signed change order, you are doing the extra work for free.
- Read your subcontract; know who can approve change orders.
- Use your own form if you have to.
- Request additional time to compete your scope if the extra work from the change order will make your original completion date impossible.

CHAPTER 15

───

ASSIGNMENTS

"I had no idea that subbing out my work would put me in default under my subcontract," Lily from Metal Works Subcontractor told me.

Lily received a notice of default letter from the general contractor saying that she needed to return to the project within forty-eight hours to complete her scope of work. The general contractor had not approved the subcontractor she had hired to do it for her. Lily is a very talented metal artist and was hired because of her talent. Lily got busy, however, and decided to hire a friend of hers, who was also a metal artist, for this project. Unfortunately, the owner did not like her friend's work and demanded that Lily return to the project. Lily's subcontract had a provision that stated she could not sub out her work unless the general contractor approved the new metal artist first.

This clause is referred to as an "anti-assignment clause," and they are in most subcontracts.

Changing the anti-assignment clauses in your subcontract is necessary if you plan to hire a subcontractor to do your work. On the other hand, a clause that tries to stop you from factoring your invoices cannot be enforced against you. This is another type of anti-assignment clause. This means that the general contractor cannot stop you from factoring your invoices, although that might be a bad idea for different reasons. Factoring an invoice is selling your right to payment from the invoice for less than face value to get cash now instead of waiting for the general contractor to pay you.

TWO TYPES OF ASSIGNMENTS

Normally, in a subcontract, there will be a paragraph that deals with assignments. There are two different types of assignments generally addressed in these types of paragraphs. First is the subcontractor's ability to assign its work, meaning its ability to hire someone else to do its work. In my experience, most subcontracts do not allow the subcontractor to sub its work to another party without the general contractor's prior written consent.

The paragraph will normally look something like this:

It is expressly understood and agreed that Subcontractor's responsibilities and obligations in the Subcontract are non-delegable personal services, that the Subcontractor shall not assign responsibility for performance nor subcontract the Subcontract or any part thereof without first obtaining the written consent of Contractor. In the event such consent is given, the assignee or delegate shall be bound by the terms and conditions of this Subcontract. Any such consent to assign or delegate given by the Contractor shall not constitute a waiver of the provisions of this Subcontract with respect to any subsequent assignments or delegations of Work. No assignee or delegate shall assign responsibility for performance of the Subcontract Work assigned or delegated to it without first obtaining the written consent of Contractor.

Or it may look this:

Subcontractor will not assign its Work or any obligations under this subcontract without the General Contractor's prior written consent. Any assignment or substitution without the prior written consent of the General Contractor is void.

If you plan to sub out your work or any portion of it, negotiate this provision in the subcontract before you enter into the subcontract. You can change it to say that you have the right to assign your work and will still be 100% responsible for the performance and quality of the work. Here is an example:

> *The Subcontractor has the right to assign their Work and obligations under this subcontract. The Subcontractor remains 100% responsible for all of the Work and obligations required under the subcontract. They will also be responsible for the material suppliers, assignees, and whomever they hire.*

UNENFORCEABLE CLAUSES

The second type of assignment addressed in these types of paragraphs prohibits subcontractors from assigning their rights to payment under the subcontract. Using Lily's example mentioned earlier, Lily would assign not only the work but the right to payment as well. The general contractor could not stop Lily from assigning her right to payment under the subcontract to her friend. The general contractor would not have an obligation to pay Lily's friend, but Lily would.

These two types of assignments are not related; they are just both referred to as assignments. What this type of assignment clause is attempting to prevent is a subcontractor's ability to sell their right to payment for work done on the project. Here is an example:

Super Fireproofing Subcontractor was in a real cash crunch, and they needed to make payroll for the week but didn't have the funds. Sub submitted a pay application for work done on a school project, but it would be weeks before they were paid for that. Super Fireproofing Subcontractor thus decided to take their pay application for the school project in the amount of $30,000 to Super Subcontractor Factoring Company.

A factoring company is like a check-cashing place. They will give the subcontractor cash now and get paid by the general contractor later. Super Subcontractor Factoring Company's business of purchasing subcontractors' rights to payment for work under a subcontract. The subcontractor sells its right to payment under the subcontract to The Subcontractor sells its right to payment under the subcontract to the factoring company and gets its money now. The factoring company pays the subcontractor immediately. Factoring company waits the thirty days (at least) to be paid by the general contractor. Super Subcontractor Factoring Company makes money by paying the subcontractor less than what they are owed but then collects the full amount from the general contractor later. Factoring Company gave $27,000 to Super Fireproofing Subcontractor, who sold their right to payment for that pay application to Factoring Company. So, Factoring Company will make $3,000 (10% of the total pay application) for waiting to get paid by the general contractor for Super Fireproofing Subcontractor's work.

When Super Fireproofing Subcontractor was not paid, Factoring Company called the general contractor to demand payment of the pay application. As you would imagine, the general contractor was less than excited to receive such a phone call and declared Super Fireproofing Subcontractor in default of the subcontract because it contained the following statement.

Subcontractor may not assign or attempt to assign any funds accrued or to be accrued under the Subcontract without first obtaining the written consent of Contractor, and no such assignment shall be binding on the Contractor unless or until accepted in writing by Contractor.

After Super Fireproofing Subcontractor brought the notice of default letter to my office, I drafted a response that Super Fireproofing Subcontractor was not in default. Any provision that attempts to forbid subcontractors from selling and/or factoring their right to payment is against the law and not enforceable. Although the general contractor was not happy about the situation, they withdrew the notice of default letter. Super Fireproofing Subcontractor was back in good standing and continued with the project.

The provision could also look like this:

Subcontractor will not assign any funds accrued or to be accrued under this subcontract, and no such assignment will be binding on General Contractor.

Although your subcontract cannot stop you from factoring and/or selling your right to payment on a project, it could be a bad idea for other reasons. For example, it cost Super Fireproofing Subcontractor 10% of the amount they were owed to get the cash immediately. If Fireproofing Sub did not make more than a 10% profit on their work, they would not have enough money to pay for what the work cost them. In other words, if it cost Fireproofing Sub $28,000 to do the work that is reflected in the pay application they just sold to Factoring Company for $27,000, they would be short $1,000 and would not have enough money to pay for their labor and material. Be sure to do your math and assess whether factoring and/ or selling your right to payment on a project is worth it to you. You can quickly dig yourself into a hole you cannot get out of in this situation.

Delay damages are another way you can find yourself in a hole you don't want to be in, which we'll discuss in the next chapter.

KEY POINTS

- If you plan on hiring someone else to do your work or any portion of your work, you need to change the anti-assignment clause or get the general contractor's approval before you hire them.
- The general contractor cannot stop you from factoring or selling your rights to payment on any pay application or invoice, but doing so might be a bad idea for other reasons.

CHAPTER 16

DELAY DAMAGES

"I don't understand. Why is it going to cost me $10,000 for being ten days late finishing my work?" Pablo from Super Plumbing Subcontractor asked me.

Pablo had received a retainage payment on a project, but it was $10,000 short. Attached to the check was a deductive change order—$1,000 per day for finishing the project ten days later than promised in the schedule.

Unfortunately, after reviewing his subcontract documents (discussed in chapter 2), Pablo had agreed to finish his scope of work on a certain date and failed to do so. This is why the schedule that is submitted or agreed to is so very important. If you finish your work after the date specified, there could be a daily fee enforced, which could very rapidly eat away at the money you are owed.

There wasn't much Pablo (nor I) could do. He was out $10,000, despite putting in the time, energy, and effort to complete his scope of work.

WHAT ARE DELAY DAMAGES?

More than anything, an owner wants to know how long their project will take to complete and the exact date they can start using the building. This is because when the project is complete, it becomes something that can produce income instead of being an expense. Knowing this date is critical to the owner, whether it is the owner's scheduled grand opening or the day the owner can begin collecting rent. To nail down a completion date from the general contractor, the owner will include a penalty clause in the contract with the general contractor. This clause states that the project will be finished on an exact date—for example, June 1, 2021. If the project is not completed by that date, there is a daily charge that is taxed against any amounts owed to the general contractor for each day the project is not complete. These are delay damages, also sometimes referred to as "liquidated damages."

Where does the general contractor get the estimate for the amount of time the project will take? From the subcontractors. So, when you give a time estimate in your bid to the general contractor, be realistic. Committing to a time frame that you cannot honor will only end up costing you money.

Just as the general contractor has a daily penalty for each day the project is late, this same provision will also be included in each subcontract—even if it is not expressly outlined in the subcontract. If the prime contract has this daily rate penalty and the terms of the prime contract are incorporated into the subcontract, you will be responsible for the penalty as well. You need to check both the subcontract and the prime contract for the delay damages provision.

If you sign a change order that makes the date you agreed to have your work completed no longer possible, you need the change order to move your promised completion date as well. If you do not change the completion date, you will be held to the date you originally promised. It does not matter if it should be obvious that this extra work will take extra time. Get approval in writing.

PROVISION LANGUAGE EXAMPLES

Here are some examples of delay damage provisions and some suggestions on how to negotiate them:

LIQUIDATED DAMAGES. General Contractor will assess delay damages against Subcontractor for each calendar *day that any part of the Work remains incomplete after the expiration of the time set for the completion of the project in the Prime Contract. Subcontractor shall be responsible for $1,200.00 per day for each day that its Work remains incomplete past the completion date in the Prime Contract. General Contractor shall have sole discretion on when Subcontractor's Work is determined to be complete.*

A few things to point out here: If you have no idea when the promised completion date is, you need to request a copy of the prime contract to determine this date or change it to be the schedule agreed to in the subcontract. The other thing that needs to be changed is who has the say on when your work is complete.

Here is what a better version would look like:

LIQUIDATED DAMAGES. General Contractor will assess delay damages against Subcontractor for each calendar day that any part of Subcontractor's Work remains incomplete after the promised completion date reflected in the schedule attached to the subcontract. Subcontractor shall be responsible for $1,200.00 per day for each day that its Work remains incomplete past the completion date in the subcontract. Subcontractor is considered to be complete when all Work in Subcontractor's scope documents is completed.

Here is another problematic example:

> *COMMENCEMENT AND COMPLETION OF THE WORK: Subcontractor shall be liable for any liquidated damages, which may become due to the owner under the Prime Contract, or any expenses incurred by General Contractor (overhead and/or supervision) due to Subcontractor's delays.*

Once again, we have no idea what the completion date is or what amount of liquated damages may be assessed, so we need to see the prime contract to figure this out. Ask for a copy of the prime contract to understand what you are agreeing to.

Here is how you can fix it:

> *COMMENCEMENT AND COMPLETION OF THE WORK: Subcontractor shall be liable for any liquidated damages, which may become due to the owner under the Prime Contract, or any expenses incurred by General Contractor (overhead and/or supervision) due to Subcontractor not completing in accordance with the schedule attached to the subcontract.*

You will still need to see a copy of the prime contract to view the amount of delay damages, but now the date is based upon what is in your subcontract.

SUBCONTRACTOR DELAY DAMAGES

What about additional charges you may incur that are not your fault? For example, the general contractor calls you out to the job site, you have your scaffold delivered, and all of your guys show up. You are at the project for a few hours when the project manager shows up and says he is not ready for you. This then happens five more times before you can begin the project. You have thousands of dollars in mobilization and demobilization expenses, which were not your fault. The project manager told you to be at the site or you would be fired. Can you be reimbursed for these extra expenses? Generally speaking, no. Most subcontracts have a provision that will not let you recover these expenses even if they are not your fault.

They normally look something like this:

> *General Contractor shall not be liable to Subcontractor for any extra expenses the Subcontractor may incur because of delays caused by the General Contractor or any other person or event. In no event ever shall the General Contractor be responsible to Subcontractor for any extra expenses that Subcontractor may incur because of any delay caused by the owner or General Contractor.*

These provisions should be removed if possible; the general contractor must have some responsibility if their actions cause you to lose money. If they don't agree to remove them, ask for a change order before you do anything that costs you money and is the fault of the general contractor or another subcontractor.

Just as subcontractors need a complete understanding of delay damages, you also need to understand warranties, which we will cover in the next chapter.

KEY POINTS

- When you agree to or provide a schedule, make sure it is realistic and something you can complete.
- Search both your subcontract and the prime contract for the delay damages provision; negotiate if possible.
- For any changes in work that will take longer than your promised completion date, make sure you get approval in writing for the extra time.
- Any additional cost that is not your fault will not be recoverable unless you change the provision or ask for a change order before the cost is incurred.

CHAPTER 17

WARRANTIES

What does "warranty" mean? Well, according to Dictionary.com, a warranty is a "written guarantee, issued to the purchaser of an article by its manufacture, promising to repair or replace it if necessary within a specified period."

A warranty extends your potential liability on a project. What is required by the warranty and the length of the warranty needs to be figured into the price of your work. Waiting to consider how much a warranty might cost until someone makes a warranty claim is too late.

IMPLIED AND EXPRESS WARRANTIES

Just by the fact that you are working, the law builds in some general warranties, whether you issue a written warranty or not. The law says you have the duty to do a good job and use quality materials. You have this duty regardless. This is referred to as an "implied warranty."

A written warranty is referred to as an "express warranty." Most subcontracts contain an express warranty that tells you the type of warranty you are required to issue at the end of the project.

When a project is complete, the general contractor issues the owner a detailed warranty for a certain amount of time after the project is complete. The warranty that the general contractor issues to the owner is based on all of the subcontractors' warranties that have been issued to the general contractor. When the general contractor gets a warranty call from the owner, they pick up the phone and call the subcontractor that was responsible for that work and tell them to come fix the issue, or the owner will call the subcontractor directly.

KNOW WHAT WARRANTY IS REQUIRED

You should know the warranty that you will be required to issue when you are bidding the project. Your projected cost of any warranty work should be included in your bid. If the length of the warranty is not included within your bid package, ask the general contractor what the warranty requirement will be.

Remember that manufacturers of materials issue warranties on their products. Make sure you include the manufacturers' written warranty in any warranty packet you submit to the general contractor.

Before you sign a subcontract, you need to make sure the warranty you are agreeing to is the same one that was included in the bid package. You will need to check in two different places for the subcontract warranty requirements. First, you must check the subcontract itself for its warranty requirements. Second, if the prime contract has been made part of the subcontract, you will need to review the prime contract warranty requirements in order to make sure they are what you agreed to.

Here is an example of what a warranty provision normally looks like:

> *Subcontractor, in addition to all warranties contained and required by the Prime Contract, warrants and guarantees that its Work is in conformance with the Prime Contract, this subcontract, and all other contract documents. Subcontractor will provide all required maintenance of its Work until the project is complete and accepted by the owner. For at least one year after the owner accepts the project, Subcontractor will perform any corrective Work without cost as directed by the General Contractor.*

There are two big things that stand out here. First, this provision incorporates whatever warranty is in the prime contract, so make sure you request and read the prime contract. Second, the warranty you are issuing begins on the date the owner accepts the project, not when you completed your work. Depending on when your work is required during the project, your warranty could begin years after you completed your work.

Here is another tricky example:

> Subcontractor shall, before final payment is required, provide all warranties required by the Prime Contract. In addition, Subcontractor agrees, at its own expense, to replace or repair any faulty or defective material or Work within one year from the day of the notice of completion of the project. Subcontractor will also be responsible for the replacement or repair of any other Work that is damaged by its faulty or defective material or work.

We see in this example that the warranty you will be required to provide is again defined in the prime contract, so read it and know what it says. Normally, your insurance will cover any work that was damaged by any of your work that turns out to be faulty or defective. Depending on the cost of the repair, it may cost you less just to pay to fix the surrounding work than to file on your insurance.

DO I HAVE TO ISSUE A WARRANTY IF I REMAIN UNPAID?

Most subcontracts require that a warranty be issued with the final pay application, meaning at the very least, you have not been paid retainage. How can you protect your company from having to respond to warranty claims? Add a line to the warranty that states, "No warranty claims will be honored until the outstanding amount of retainage has been paid." This way, you can comply with the subcontract and issue the warranty but do not to have to honor any claims until you are paid.

Another issue that needs to be fully understood before you sign a subcontract is what actions or inactions could put you in default under the terms of the subcontract and how to avoid termination, which is the focus of the next chapter.

KEY POINTS

- Know what warranty will be required when you are bidding the project so you can include a projected price for any warranty claims.
- Your manufacturer issues a warranty as well; make sure you get a copy of the written warranty to include with your warranty packet submitted to the general contractor.
- Make sure the warranty required by the subcontract and the prime contract is the same one you reviewed in your bid.
- Add a restriction to you warranty if you are required to issue one before you are paid.

CHAPTER 18

———

DEFAULT AND TERMINATION

"But I'll lose all the money I spent getting ready for this job if they terminate me now," Jessy from Super Wall Covering Subcontractor gasped.

Jessy received a notice of termination email for a project she had not started yet. Jessy signed the subcontract ninety days ago and was supposed to start next week. To prepare for the project, she had already ordered $10,000 worth of the specific wall covering the project called for.

The wall covering Jessy ordered was custom made and could not be returned. Now all of that money would be lost.

Unfortunately, Jessy's subcontract contained a termination for convenience clause. A termination for convenience clause states that the general contractor could fire Jessy's company for any reason at any time without any notice. Jessy, on the other hand, did not have the same right to terminate the contract. Jessy was terminated because the general contractor had found a different subcontractor who would do the work for less than what Jessy charged.

Termination for the convenience clause is bullshit and should be removed—or, at the very least, be mutual.

WHAT ARE DEFAULT AND TERMINATION CLAUSES?

A termination for convenience clause allows the general contractor to terminate your subcontract without any notice. This is what happened to Jessy. The other type of termination clauses found in subcontracts are termination for cause, meaning you have failed to comply with the subcontract in some way. You are in default when you fail to comply with the terms of the subcontract. Usually, if you are in default under the subcontract, the general contractor will send you notice that you are in default. If you fail to fix the default, the general contractor can then terminate you and your subcontract. Know what your subcontract says about when you are in default and the time you have to fix the default.

Make sure what happened to Jessy does not happen to you. The first thing we need to address is the termination for convenience clause.

Here is an example of what it looks like.

TERMINATION OF SUBCONTRACTOR FOR CONVENIENCE. General Contractor may, at any time, by written notice to Subcontractor, terminate Subcontractor in whole or part or any portion of its Work required under the subcontract, without cause, whenever the General Contractor, in its sole discretion, determines that such termination is necessary. Such termination shall not prejudice any other rights General Contractor has under this subcontract.

Or here is another example:

TERMINATION OF THE SUBCONTRACT FOR CONVENIENCE: General Contractor may, without cause, terminate Subcontractor in whole or part. General Contractor will give Subcontractor written notice of such termination. Subcontractor will be paid for any Work performed; if Subcontractor had not started Work at the project, Subcontractor is not entitled to any payment.

Remove these provisions; they serve no purpose other than offering an easy out for the general contractor if they find someone else to do your work for cheaper. This provision is completely one-sided, and you are taking a huge risk by signing a subcontract with this language.

Once you sign the subcontract, you are on the hook to do the work. If you don't do the work and it costs the general contractor more than what you agreed to do the work for, you are responsible for covering the increase in cost. This can be avoided if you include having the right to terminate for convenience as well.

WHEN ARE YOU CONSIDERED TO BE IN DEFAULT?

The subcontract will specifically address when you are considered to be in default. Below are the most common elements defining "default" that I have seen.

- Failed to proceed with the work as directed by the general contractor.
- Failed to prosecute work diligently, including the failure to provide sufficient numbers of skilled workers or proper materials and failure to adhere to the schedule.
- Caused delay or disruption to the general contractor or other subcontractors.
- Failed to perform any requirement of the subcontract.
- Filed bankruptcy.
- Performed work in a manner that is rejected by the owner and/or architect.

You must do good work in a timely manner in order to avoid being considered in default, which does not seem unreasonable. However, who gets to decide if you are working "diligently" enough? Answer: the general contractor.

Each email they send to you saying you need to work faster or have more guys will be considered as a default, and all of those documents can and will be used against you. Make sure you immediately respond to any emails or letters complaining of your work in writing. A notice of default does not have to specifically say "notice of default." It does not have to be sent via certified mail or from an attorney. It can be from any project manager or anyone who works for the general contractor or owner. Any email, text, or any other way of communication that states you are not doing your job or you are doing it incorrectly is a notice of default and needs an immediate response.

You agreed to do everything that is in the subcontract, including all the small things like daily reports, turning your pay apps in on time, and signing the required lien waivers. Failure to do any of those things can put you in default. The general contractor may not say anything at the time but will use it later to say you defaulted on the subcontract.

I'M IN DEFAULT. NOW WHAT?

What happens when you are in default? The subcontract will normally call for some amount of time to fix your default. For example, *Upon forty-eight hours of written notice of the default, Subcontractor shall at its own expense cure the default. If Subcontractor fails to cure the defaults set forth in the written notice, General Contractor may terminate Subcontractor upon written notice of such termination.* This means that you have forty-eight hours to fix whatever the general contractor's notice says is wrong.

You need to respond immediately to a notice of default. The response needs to be in writing and must state either the reasons that you disagree and why you are not in default, or the immediate action you are taking to fix the default.

I'VE BEEN TERMINATED. NOW WHAT?

What happens if you are terminated? Nothing very good. First, payment for work you have already completed will be withheld until your scope of work is completed. When your scope of work is completed, if it has not cost the general contractor more than your subcontract amount to complete your work, you will be paid any remaining amount. In all of my years working in construction law, I have never seen a subcontractor paid any amount after they were terminated. When you are terminated, the general contractor now has to go hire someone else to complete your work. The general contractor will not owe you any money if the replacement subcontractor costs more than you agreed to do the work.

In fact, once you are terminated, the general contractor has the right to come after you for any amount it spends over the amount they agreed to pay you. Normally, the subcontract will allow the general contractor to add 10% or 15% onto the amount of the replacement subcontractor for their overhead and time they have to spend finding your replacement. That provision normally looks something like this: *Upon termination General Contractor at Subcontractor's expense plus 10% for General Contractor's time and overhead fees, hire any replacement Subcontractor it deems necessary.*

Make sure you immediately fix any issues that the general contractor has addressed in a notice of default. It is also best to respond to these notices in writing with how you plan to fix the problem.

Jessy lost $10,000 because she did not remove the termination for convenience provision from her subcontract. Do not let it cost you money. Make sure you remove this provision from the next subcontract you sign.

Another issue that could bring an unexpected cost are

attorney fees. I will address how to limit your paying attorney fees in the next chapter.

KEY POINTS

- Never agree to a termination for convenience provision. Or at least make it mutual.
- Be familiar with all the requirements of the subcontract; failing to follow any of them will cause you to be in default.
- Know how long you have to fix a default.
- Respond immediately and in writing to any notice of default.
- At all costs, fix the defect and avoid being terminated. You will not be paid for any work already done, and you will be responsible for the expense and cost of the replacement subcontractor.

CHAPTER 19

ATTORNEY FEES AND COSTS

"The general contractor did not pay me on time. Why do I have to pay my material supplier's attorney fees? I cannot pay them because the general contractor has not paid me yet," Holly from Super Stucco Subcontractor explained to me.

The first thing I had to explain to Holly is that according to her subcontract, the general contractor does not have to pay her until they are paid by the owner. Unfortunately, she does not have that type of agreement with her material suppliers or the people who work for her.

Every Friday, she owes her team a paycheck whether she received payment from the general contractor or not. The same is true for her material suppliers; their bills are due in thirty days whether she was paid or not. Further, if Holly does not pay her material suppliers and they take steps to collect their money, she is responsible for the cost associated with those efforts.

I drafted a paragraph that Holly could add to her subcontracts from here on out, which will allow her to be reimbursed for any cost and attorney fees she is forced to spend because the general contractor did not pay her on time. See the next section for a paragraph you can use.

You need to make sure that your subcontracts have a provision for attorney fees and that it allows you to recover your legal expenses.

If your subcontract does not have a provision that deals with attorney fees and costs, you may not be able to recover them. If the subcontract is silent as to the ability to recover attorney fees, you have to use the state laws that deal with attorney fees in order to recover them. If you were to sue a general contractor who did not pay you, you would sue them for breach of the subcontract. The laws that go with your claim for breach of the contract say that you can recover your fees, even if the agreement about fees is not in writing, but you have to give thirty days' written notice before you file suit. The notice must state what you are suing them for and that you will be seeking recovery of your attorney fees. If you have a provision in your subcontract dealing with attorney fees, you do not have to send this notice.

Another major issue is that under the current state of the law in Texas, if you sue an entity that is a Limited Liability Company (LLC) for breach of contract and you do not have a written provision in your contract dealing with attorney fees, you will not be able to recover them. Meaning if you have to sue a general contractor because they did not pay you, the general contractor is an LLC, and you do not have a written provision calling for attorney fees, you cannot recover your attorney fees.

PROVISION LANGUAGE EXAMPLES

Below is a general attorney fee provision I normally find in subcontracts that needs to be altered:

In the event of a default or defaults by Subcontractor, General Contractor shall be entitled to recover all costs, damages, and expenses incurred by General Contractor. General Contractor shall also be entitled to recover all costs, expenses, and fees, including reasonable and necessary attorney fees incurred as a result of Subcontractor's default.

Here is another problematic example:

If General Contractor is required to employ an attorney to enforce any provision hereof, or to collect damages for breach of the subcontract, Subcontractor agrees to reimburse General Contractor for such reasonable and necessary attorney fees and all other costs that General Contractor may incur or expend in connection with any such default.

The following should be added to both of these provisions to make sure you can recover your attorney fees and costs as well:

General Contractor shall reimburse Subcontractor for any and all costs and attorney fees Subcontractor shall incur as a result of any default of the General Contractor of any portion of this subcontract or the prime contract. General Contractor shall also be responsible for any collection costs and/or attorney fees that Subcontractor is required to pay its material suppliers and/or labors because General Contractor did not pay Subcontractor in a timely manner in accordance with the subcontract.

DON'T BE FORCED TO WALK AWAY

Bart, a painting subcontractor came into my office because he was owed $15,000 from a remodeling contractor he had worked for. He was owed the $15,000 for three different projects, but we could not file liens because they were all homesteads and the procedure to file a lien was not followed.

The contractor who hired him was an LLC, and they did not have an agreement in writing. I told Bart it would be worth a few hundred dollars for me to make some phone calls and send a demand letter, but it would not be worth filing suit to collect because he could not get his attorney fees back.

Also, once he filed suit, he opened himself up to counterclaims and thousands of dollars in litigation costs even if he didn't do anything wrong.

I made the calls and sent the letter, but in that case, the best business decision he could make was to walk away from the money he was owed and learn the lesson: you always need a written agreement and one that has a provision for attorney fees.

Another benefit of having a written agreement is you can address in advance how disputes will be handled. This is what we will cover in the next chapter: dispute resolution.

KEY POINTS

- You have to pay your team and your material suppliers even if you have not been paid by the general contractor.
- Have a written subcontract that has provisions dealing with attorney fees.
- Make sure the attorney fee provision lets you recover your fees as well.

CHAPTER 20

DISPUTE RESOLUTION

I cannot think of a way to make this topic sexy and exciting, but it is something you need to know and understand.

Disputes will arise. You need to know your options because it will be key in resolving these issues. There are three formal ways to resolve disputes when you cannot do it on your own: mediation, courtroom litigation, and arbitration. I will explain what all three are and the pros and cons of each.

MEDIATION

Mediation is when the parties in a dispute come together to see if they can settle their differences before going to court. During mediation, there is no determination of who is right or who is wrong. There is no judgment issued. A good mediation is when both parties leave pissed off, but the case is settled.

Normally, a mediation is held on neutral ground at the mediator's office. The mediator is normally an attorney who is familiar with your type of case but is not involved in the case and has no interest in the case's outcome. Mediation usually starts with all the parties and their attorneys sitting around a table glaring at each other. The mediator will then come in and explain the ground rules and the mediation process. When the mediator is complete, each side will get a chance to explain their side of the story respectfully and without interruption.

Despite how fair and structured this sounds, mediation is an intense experience. When it's your turn to speak, it feels good because everyone has to listen to your side of the story. (The attorney normally tells the story, but the client can if they feel comfortable.) When it's the other party's time to speak, however, it is like listening to nails on a chalkboard. It feels like they are tearing your good name apart and questioning your credibility.

Although intense and often uncomfortable, this opening session is tremendously helpful. You get to hear exactly what the other side's arguments are—which will generally be the same arguments they present in litigation if the case does not settle. After each side has had a chance to tell their story, the parties then go to separate rooms. The mediator will go back and forth between the rooms, bringing in offers and the most compelling evidence available in an attempt to have each side seriously evaluate their case and settle the matter.

This is a chance to look at your case honestly with all of the holes and risks. There is no such thing as a perfect slam-dunk case, and anyone who tells you that one exists is lying to you. Attorneys are good at their job and will always find holes or create them. This is the last time that you have any say in the outcome of your case. If you do not settle at mediation, the outcome of your case will be decided by a judge, jury, or arbitrator where you have no control. That is the same as taking all of the money you spent on the case and going to the casino.

If you are unable to settle your dispute via mediation, you are left with the two options: courtroom litigation or arbitration, one of which will be in your subcontract. Know which one would work best for you, and make sure that is the option that is in your subcontract.

COURTROOM LITIGATION

If you chose courtroom litigation, that means your dispute will be decided by the public court system, where a judge or a jury will make a decision, and a judgment will be issued.

The process normally goes something like this: you file a lawsuit, which normally costs anywhere from $300 to $600. You'll then spend at least a year waiting to get to trial. During that year (or years) waiting to go to trial, the discovery process will take place. This is where you have to answer questions both in writing and in person and turn over every document you have on the matter, and most times, you will also be required to produce documents that do not even relate to the matter. It is an invasive and expensive process.

When it is your turn to go to trial, each side will present their opening statements, sharing the story of the case and what they think the evidence will prove. Then the plaintiff (the party that filed suit first) will present their evidence. Evidence is presented through witnesses, through their statements and the document(s) that they have to help prove their story. The defendant (the party being sued) will cross-examine the plaintiff's witnesses and try to discredit them in order to prove that they are lying. Then the defendant will present their case, and the plaintiff gets to cross-examine their witnesses.

In the court system, there are many rules to determine

what evidence will be considered and many rules on how it can be presented. Once both parties have had a chance to present their evidence, they each present a closing argument. This is their story of why and what they should win. When both parties are done, the judge or the jury will consider all of the evidence and arguments made by the attorneys and make a decision. The jury will start its deliberations and will keep deliberating until it has reached a verdict and a judgment will be issued. If there is not a jury, the judge will consider the evidence and arguments of the attorneys and, depending on the judge, will issue a judgment at the close of the case or weeks to months later.

Pros of courtroom litigation: there is a low filing fee, and your case is decided by a jury of your peers. Cons: it will be at least a year to get your case to trial, there is an the expensive discovery process, and not all evidence is allowed at trial.

ARBITRATION

The other option is arbitration. The process is similar to the courtroom, but an arbitrator makes the decision instead of a judge or a jury.

An arbitrator is normally an attorney who is experienced in your type of case. When you file your claim in arbitration, with the arbitration company that is named in the subcontract, they will send a packet with at least ten potential arbitrators who are not related to either party in the case. Each party then reviews each arbitrator's résumé and experience, strikes the ones they do not like, and ranks their top five. The arbitration company compares both lists and picks the one that is most liked by the parties to be the arbitrator.

The discovery period is limited, and all documents and evidence will be considered at trial. Normally, you can get to an arbitration hearing in around six months. The availability is based on the parties' schedules. The cons to arbitration: it is expensive to file, normally around $3,000 per party, and you have to pay the arbitrator an hourly rate for their time. Another thing to consider is that an arbitration award cannot be easily appealed, so you are stuck with the decision you get.

PROVISION LANGUAGE EXAMPLES

Mediation is a good idea before you go to court or file an arbitration, so I recommend including it in your subcontract. The provisions in subcontracts that deal with dispute resolution are all over the board, but most prefer arbitration because initially it is more expensive, which will deter most subcontractors from filing claims. I have provided two written clauses for you: one for the courtroom and one for arbitration. Use whatever clause works best for you.

For courtroom use:

Any claim arising out of or related to this Subcontract shall be subject to litigation in the district Court where the project is located. If it is a federal project, litigation will be brought in the proper federal court where the project is located. Before either party can file a suit for litigation, the parties must mediate. The party wishing to file litigation must send the other party a demand for mediation within 60 days of the date of the demand. If the other party refuses to go to mediation within the 60 days, the mediation requirement is waived and the party can file its claim in litigation.

For arbitration use:

Any claim arising out of or related to this subcontract shall be subject to arbitration at American Arbitration Association, under the construction industry rules. Before either party can file for arbitration, the parties must mediate. The party wishing to file arbitration must send the other party a demand for mediation within 60 days to respond to the demand. If the other party refuses to go to mediation within the 60 days, the mediation requirement is waived and the party can file its claim in *arbitration. The parties agree it will be a one-arbitrator panel, and each party shall pay no more than $200.00 per hour for the arbitrator's time.*

AVOID LITIGATION IF POSSIBLE

I am going to be honest with you: the only people who win in the courtroom or arbitration are the attorneys—and I say this as an attorney. An attorney is paid by the hour, so they get to keep billing you if you do not settle. They are the ones who will make money in litigation, not you, and the best you can hope for is to break even. The parties can settle at any time, and the quicker they do, the more money they will both save.

I have taken many cases to trial and arbitration, and if you are in business to make money and grow your company, this is not where you want to be. The hundreds, if not thousands, of hours of your time spent on a case that is in ligation are better spent on growing your company. The stress of dealing with litigation will take years off your life. Can you imagine having other attorneys asking you any questions they want and you have to answer? The truth will be stretched into something you do not recognize. They will only tell half of the story, and it is not uncommon for the parties and the attorneys to flat out lie and be misleading.

The attorney fees will reach at least $100,000 if you have to go to trial, and the best you could hope for is to break even. *Principle in litigation never makes business sense.* I am not saying you should back down from a fight; especially if you are sued, you must defend yourself. But you need to make sure you have a fighting chance, and that starts with having a fair subcontract (which is the whole purpose of this book).

As most subcontracts stand now, even if you did all your work correctly, you could still be sued, and you would lose because they are written so unfairly. There are general contractors out there who sue subcontractors with the complete expectation that they will not answer the lawsuit, and the general contractor will get a judgment against the subcontractor by default. If the subcontractor does answer, the general contractor will litigate them out of court. In most cases, the general contractor usually wins because the subcontractor cannot afford to defend themselves.

So, do yourself a favor and avoid litigation altogether— and that starts with understanding everything in your subcontract.

KEY POINTS

- There are three ways to formally settle a dispute: mediation, court-room, or arbitration.
- If your case goes to court, the best outcome you can hope for is to break even.
- Know what your subcontract says about dispute resolution, and use whatever provision works best for you.

CONCLUSION

No one goes into a project expecting it to go wrong, but it does happen.

Sometimes, the projects that go wrong cause financial hardship, and you lose money. In worst-case scenarios, damages can be so bad that your company goes out of business. This, to me, is the most heartbreaking—when thousands of hours of people's lives and effort, sometimes generations of work, end because of one fucked-up job.

But you don't have to worry as much about that anymore. You are now equipped to properly evaluate risks, negotiate your next subcontract, and quit getting screwed!

Let's quickly review the risks we covered with each provision. Although some provisions do not present a risk, we discussed helpful tips you should implement—even if they are not required by your subcontract.

- **Chapter 1—The Bid:** A bid that underestimates the cost of the project can be accepted, and you will have to do the work at a loss.
- **Chapter 2—Subcontract Documents:** Your bid is not included in the subcontract documents; your work is only defined by the scope described in the subcontract. Do not agree to a contract you have never seen. Do not agree that the prime contract will be part of your subcontract.
- **Chapter 3—Subcontractor Bonds:** Providing a bond is risking all of your personal assets to work on a project.
- **Chapter 4—Scope of Work:** The scope has most likely changed since your bid. Do not agree to work that was not in your bid. Read and review the scope described in the subcontract as if it were a new bid package.
- **Chapter 5—Do Not Sign a Personal Guarantee:** Signing a personal guarantee is another way that your personal assets will be at risk for a construction project.
- **Chapter 6—Prior Work and Field Conditions:** You will be responsible for the work of the subcontractor before you. Visit the project site before you sign the subcontract.

- **Chapter 7—Submittals and As Builts:** A tool to say that your material and work were agreed to with no issues. If this is not in your subcontract, you should do it anyway.
- **Chapter 8—Daily Reports:** A great way to tell your side of the story as it happens. If this is not in your subcontract, do it anyway.
- **Chapter 9—Pay When Paid Clauses:** You have to wait for the owner to pay the general contractor before you are paid, an event you have no control over. Doing a good job on time is not enough to be paid.
- **Chapter 10—Retainage:** Retainage can limit the owner's liability to lien claimants.
- **Chapter 11—When Can I File a Lien?** You can file a lien even if your subcontract says you cannot. You can file a lien early, but you cannot be late.
- **Chapter 12—Lien Waivers:** Signing an unconditional lien waiver when you have not been paid will waive your right to payment.
- **Chapter 13—Trust Funds:** The funds you are paid for a project must be used to pay for the labor and material on that project.
- **Chapter 14—Change Orders:** If extra work is not approved in writing, you will not be paid for it.
- **Chapter 15—Assignments:** You can't sub out your work without prior approval.
- **Chapter 16—Delay Damages:** Not completing your work on time could cost you anywhere from

$500–$1,000(depending on the contract) for each day you are late.

- **Chapter 17—Warranties:** Your warranty does not start until the whole project is complete. How long is the warranty period?
- **Chapter 18—Default and Termination:** You can be fired for any reason at any time.
- **Chapter 19—Attorney Fees and Costs:** You may not be able to recover any attorney fees you have to pay to enforce the subcontract.
- **Chapter 20—Dispute Resolution:** Do you want a courtroom or an arbitrator to decide your case?

Now, put what you've learned into practice. Go grab the last subcontract you signed (or the one you are about to sign), and find each provision in this book. Read each provision and consider the risk you are taking.

If you are willing to take the risk, you do not have to do anything. Conducting any type of business is a risk. Being informed of what the risks are before you agree to take them is where you will find success. That is the point of this whole book. Only you can decide what risks are worth taking for your company. If you are not willing to take the risk, reread the appropriate chapter and see how to modify or remove the risk.

If you have questions or want a PDF of any of the

forms mentioned in this book, drop by my website: **SubcontractorInstitute.com**. In addition, I would love to hear how this book helped you, so send me an email at karalynn@thecromeenslawfirm.com and share your story with me!

ACKNOWLEDGMENTS

Writing this book would not have been possible without the following people.

Mom: For always telling me I could do whatever I put my mind to and giving me the two phrases required for a successful life: "Can't never did try" and "If you don't have anything nice to say, don't say anything at all."

Jess, Courtney, and Jackie: You guys have done a great job keeping everything running smoothly so I could take the time to write this book. Thank you so much for leading our winning team.

Lily Rush: You are so incredibly smart, beautiful, and talented. Thank you for reading my book and helping me edit.

ABOUT THE AUTHOR

KARALYNN CROMEENS is the founder of The Cromeens Law Firm, PLLC ("TCLF"). Founded in 2006, TCLF focuses on the complete representation of subcontractors and material suppliers. Karalynn has reviewed and negotiated thousands of subcontracts; she is on a mission to make the subcontract a fair document. The first step on this mission is to teach subcontractors what the terms of the subcontract mean and the risk involved with the terms so they can make informed decisions before the subcontract is signed. When Karalynn is not helping subcontractors and material suppliers, she enjoys spending time with her husband, Brad, and three daughters: Lily, Holly, and Jessy.

Made in the USA
Las Vegas, NV
09 November 2022

59088938R00114